DOGS OF DESTINY

TO
THE K-9 CORPS AND MARINE WAR DOGS
OF THE SECOND WORLD WAR

This edition published 2023
by Living Book Press

ISBN: 978-1-922919-12-0 (hardcover)
 978-1-922919-21-2 (softcover)
 978-1-922919-22-9 (ebook)

Originally published in 1949 by Charles Scribner's Sons.

A catalogue record for this
book is available from the
National Library of Australia

DOGS OF DESTINY

BY

FAIRFAX DOWNEY

AND

PAUL BROWN

WITH PEN-AND-INK ILLUSTRATIONS BY

PAUL BROWN

Living Book Press

CONTENTS

A LEGEND OF THE DOG

Not long after the creation of the world, a crack opened in the surface of the earth. Slowly and steadily it widened. Soon it would become a broad, impassable chasm.

Man found himself on one side of the gap, with all the beasts on the other.

Alone among the animals the dog gave heed to the separation. Whining piteously, he ran along the edge. At last he sat and gazed across at the man with wistful and imploring eyes.

"Come!" called the man.

By now the chasm, dangerously wide, revealed a fearful abyss. Yet the dog never hesitated. With all his strength he jumped. He did not quite clear it, but his forelegs reached and clung to the farther side.

Quickly the man grasped the dog and drew him up to safety at his side.

"You shall be my comrade," the man declared.

So the dog ever since has remained.

DOG OF DOOM

INSTRUMENT OF FATE

THIS is a dog story written on papyrus more than 3600 years ago. It begins with a Pharoah of Egypt whose heart was grieved that no man-child had been born to him. He prayed for a son to the Hathors, the gods of time, and they granted his wish, but in the same moment pronounced the boy's doom.

"He shall die by the crocodile, or by the serpent, or by the dog."

By every means, the Pharoah strove to protect his son against his cruel destiny, keeping him in a stone tower on a mountain top, carefully guarded. Yet as the lad grew, he could no longer be confined. No sooner had he stepped into the world outside than he beheld a strange animal.

"What is that that runs behind a man walking on the road?" he asked his page.

"It is a dog," the servitor answered.

"Let one be brought me exactly like it," commanded the young Prince.

Pharoah was distraught but could not deny his son. "Let

him be given a young running dog lest his heart be saddened," he directed.

So upon the Prince was bestowed a coursing hound, one of those fleet animals--probably a Saluki--with which the Egyptians overtook the swiftest game. Not even when his father revealed the fate hanging over him could the lad be persuaded to give up his pet. The dog followed faithfully at his heels when he departed from Egypt and sought adventure in foreign lands.

The Prince, disguised as the son of a soldier of the chariots, won the hand of the beautiful daughter of the King of Naharinna from many suitors by performing the task of scaling the sheer walls of her tower, seventy cubits high. But the King, believing the Prince to be of mean birth, drove him and his bride from court.

While the Prince and his wife were dwelling in exile, he told her of the prophecy declaring that one of three animals would prove his doom. She looked at the hound, which had faithfully followed them, and begged: "Slay the dog that runs before thee." But he refused without hesitation. "I cannot slay the dog that I brought up when it was little," he said.

It was not the dog, however, but a serpent that came first to bring the Prince's fate upon him. The Princess saw the poisonous thing crawling toward her husband as he slept. Quickly she placed a bowl of milk in its path. When the snake lapped it up and grew torpid, she chopped it to bits with a hatchet.

Then came the crocodile. The huge reptile crept up from the river one night, seized the Prince in its jaws and began to drag him off. And as it crawled, it spoke to its victim:

"Behold, I am thy doom, following after thee..."

There, tantalizingly, the story breaks off, for the last part of the papyrus was destroyed by a powder explosion. But scholars have reconstructed this ending.

The valiant Princess slew the crocodile also. Now the jealous suitors set out in pursuit of their successful rival and his wife, and the young couple and their dog hid in a cave. As the suitors passed it, the dog barked a warning and betrayed the hiding place. Bravely the Prince fought his assailants, but they were too many. The Princess sacrificed herself for him, stepping in front of him to take a javelin in her breast, and the dog died, too, defending his master. Finally the Prince fell beneath the suitors' blows.

Doom was fulfilled. Satisfied, the gods restored all three to life. Such perfect devotion, they decreed, deserved to live on.

Paul Brown

ARGUS

HOUND OF ULYSSES

ULYSSES had bred the dog Argus. His trait of watchfulness, evident even in puppyhood, must have caused him to be named for the fabled giant who had a hundred eyes. When Ulysses left his island kingdom of Ithaca to join the Greek expedition against Troy, Argus was still too young to train. But the image of his master was fixed in the puppy's mind, and the memory of dogs is long.

In Ithaca, Argus, grown large and swift, coursed deer, wild goats, and hares with the huntsmen. He was no "table dog"--animals the Greeks kept as house pets-but of the strong, fierce breed used for the chase or to guard the herds and flocks.

After a siege of ten years, Troy was taken by the stratagem of the wooden horse, and Ulysses began that long voyage home which is the theme of Homer's Odyssey. It was a journey fraught with such perilous adventures that it consumed ten years more and demanded all the hero's courage and craft before he reached Ithaca.

There most believed Ulysses dead. Few besides his faithful wife Penelope still hoped. The supposed widow was only able to put off scores of importunate suitors by promising to make her choice among them when she completed a garment; all she wove by day she unraveled each night.

None knew Ulysses when he returned, disguised in a beggar's rags, but the still loyal swineherd, Eumaeus, accompanied the stranger in an invasion of the palace that would end in triumph over the suitors.

Without the gates they beheld an old dog, derelict and masterless, lying on a dung heap for warmth, his hide twitching under the torment of ticks. Argus knew Ulysses instantly. He dropped his ears forward, and his tail thumped with joy, yet he was too feeble to drag himself toward his master.

Ulysses brushed away a tear. "Eumaeus," he said, "how strange such a dog lies on a dunghill. He is beautifully formed, but I am not certain whether his speed and strength match his looks, or whether he is merely one of the table dogs their masters keep for show."

"Truly," the swineherd answered, "that is a dog of one who died in a far-off country. If his form and strength were still as they were when Ulysses departed for Troy, you would marvel at his fleetness and courage. No quarry he tracked into the depths of the forest could escape him. Now he has fallen on evil days, his master has perished in a foreign land, and neglectful women give him no more care."

Now that he had looked on the master for whom he had waited so long, the old dog's eyes closed.

"Argus the dog," Homer relates, "went down into the blackness of death, that moment he saw Ulysses after twenty years."

An epitaph, written by another Greek poet, would serve well for the faithful Argus.

"Thou who passest on this path,
If haply thou dost mark this monument,
Laugh not, I pray thee, though it is a dog's grave.
Tears fell for me, and the dust was heaped above me
By a master's hand."

Paul Brown

PERITES

HE SAVED ALEXANDER THE GREAT

BESIDES his black war horse, Bucephalus, Alexander the Great owned a celebrated dog. To man-enemy or friend--the conqueror could be ruthless. In fits of suspicion he ordered the execution of generals who had served him long and loyally. But for horse and dog, his devotion, once given, was intense and unwavering.

Perites was sent to Alexander as a gift by a monarch seeking his favor; some say the King of Albania, others King Porus of India. The dog was presented along with a scroll, declaring him to be the last of a royal breed and asking that he be tried on big game.

Except for his size and his look of dormant strength, Perites was not impressive. However, Alexander eagerly sent him into the arena. In turn, an antlered stag, a fierce wolf, and a bear were loosed against him. Perites, plainly bored, paid them no attention whatever. He yawned, lay down and went to sleep. Alexander in chagrin commanded the three animals be driven back to their cages. The apparently spiritless and sluggish dog was close to being sent home with a sharp message that no

monarch dare trifle with Alexander save at his peril. But perhaps, it occurred to the Emperor, the dog's antagonists had not
been formidable enough to interest him. He snapped another
order. Into the arena bounded a Numidian lion. The savage,
black-maned beast had killed all his previous opponents and
several keepers. He charged with a roar, and Perites sprang to
meet him. They met head on in the shock of combat. In one
minute the dog tore out the lion's throat.

Next a huge battle elephant came lumbering in. Perites'
hackles rose and he uttered a deep bay. Flinging himself at
the mighty creature, he attacked, adroitly avoiding tusks and
trunk and the ponderous feet which strove to crush him to a
pulp. Perites darted in and out, ripping at a flank. Bellowing,
the elephant spun around and around in vain attempts to reach
his assailant. Dizzy and exhausted, he toppled to the ground
with a tremendous crash and lay still. Perites stood over him,
triumphant.

Thereafter Alexander kept the dog close to his side through
all his march of conquest through Asia. Perites merited his
trust. One night an assassin slipped past the guards and stole
silently into the royal tent. He poised a dagger over the sleeping Alexander. In that moment Perites awoke, leaped for the
would-be murderer and dragged him down. But his hide was
pricked by the dagger, its point dipped in deadly poison. In
agony but with merciful swiftness, Perites expired.

The tears that Alexander shed for his dog came more truly
from the heart than those wept for "more worlds to conquer."
As he had done for his horse Bucephalus, he named a city in
his dog's honor, calling it Perite. There he endowed a temple
whose priests were commanded to offer perpetual sacrifices
to the memory of the faithful animal.

ALCIBIADES' DOG

LOYALTY UNDESERVED

CURVED and plumed was the big dog's tail, and he carried it like a banner. So magnificent was his appearance--he resembled a Newfoundland--that an Athenian sculptor portrayed him on a marble bas relief. Though the dog's name has not come down to us, Plutarch mentions him, taking special note of that gallant appendage. "And a beautiful tail it was," says the historian.

That tail wagged in utmost devotion for the dog's master: Alcibiades, brilliant general and wily politician of Athens in the great days of ancient Greece. Alcibiades was dissolute and luxurious. Scruples never stood in the way of his ambition. He betrayed his wife who had brought him a fortune. Not even the famous philosopher Socrates, his tutor, could persuade him to mend his ways. But Alcibiades' dog knew only that he loved his master.

The arrogant young Greek had paid a great sum for the dog and adorned him with a golden collar. Once five thieves set on the animal in an attempt to rob him of his precious ornament. Four of them the dog put to panic-stricken flight; the fifth he seized by his garments and dragged him home a prisoner.

Alcibiades, more proud than ever of his pet, strolled with

him through the city. Admiring citizens pointed them out. "There goes the handsomest man and the handsomest dog on earth."

But the day came when the schemes of Alcibiades and his intrigues with the Spartans and Persians began to turn the populace against him. Then he resorted to a cruel and despicable trick. He cut off his dog's fine tail at the root and led him through the city.

The poor dog, desperately ashamed of his looks yet with devotion unwavering, followed his unworthy master. At the sight of the mutilation, the Athenians cried out in furious indignation. Alcibiades only laughed. "That's just what I want," he said. "I want Athens to talk about this, that it may have nothing worse to say of me."

For a time it worked. Ultimately, the citizens cast the oyster-shell ballots that sent Alcibiades into exile. Such a man, for all his talents and victories, was better banished. Only his dog still clung to him and accompanied him to Phrygia.

There, one night in 40 B.C., Alcibiades' enemies burned the house where he lay sleeping. The exile woke to grasp his sword, wrapped his cloak around his left arm as a shield and rushed out to fight for his life. Ahead of him dashed his dog, fiercely attacking the assassins. The murderous crew fled before them. But from a distance they launched flights of javelins and arrows, piercing both their victims through and through. As Alcibiades fell slain, his dying dog crawled to his side and with his last strength tried to draw one of the missiles from the body of his master.

VIGE

COMPANION OF A VIKING

DRAGON-SHIPS beached on the coast of Ireland, and the Viking band swept through the countryside. Harried often by these dreaded Norsemen, the farm folk fled in terror. Rapidly the raiders emptied many a byre of cattle and drove them toward shore. Before the beeves could be slaughtered, a greatly daring peasant ventured out of hiding and begged the Viking leader to restore his twenty cows, all he possessed on earth.

Olaf Trygvason, Olaf I, King of Norway, stroked his beard and stared at the Gael bold enough to face him. His fierce glance lightened. "Pick and prove which cows are yours and you shall have them back," he promised, "but delay not our march." The peasant blew a blast on his horn and spoke a brief order to the shaggy shepherd dog that trotted up. Instantly the animal plunged into the milling mass of cattle. Without hesitation he singled out and herded apart exactly twenty cows. Every one of them bore the same brand mark cut in an ear.

Olaf, gesturing their owner to take them, asked:
"Will you sell me the dog?"
"I would rather give him to you," came the answer.

Paul Brown

The King accepted the gift but in return bestowed a gold ring on the peasant and pledged him friendship in the future. Declares the Icelandic saga, *Heimskringla*: "This dog was called Vige, and was the very best of dogs, and Olaf owned him long afterwards."

Vige faithfully followed his new master through the fierce conflicts which ensued when Olaf, late in the tenth century, embraced Christianity. Conversion or the sword was the choice he offered all who worshiped Odin and Thor.

Among the Norsemen who clung to the old gods was Raud the Strong, reputed able to conjure up fair winds for his fleet. In spite of his wizardry, Olaf defeated him in a sea fight. Raud drove his ship ashore and fled, hotly pursued by Olaf. The pagan chieftain, fleet of foot, was about to escape when the King shouted to his dog, "Vige ! Vige ! Catch the deer!"

After the runner sped the dog. In great bounds he overtook the fugitive, sank his teeth in a leg and halted him. Olaf, rushing up, flung a spear which transfixed his foe, but before Raud fell he dealt Vige a frightful blow with his sword.

Vige, a great wound gaping in his side, was borne back on a shield. Carefully tended, he recovered and took part in Olaf's last great battle.

The might of the heathen Kings of Sweden and Denmark, joined against him, overwhelmed the Christian King of Norway Olaf, fighting to the end on the deck of his ship, *Long Serpent*, vanished overboard, never to be seen again. Einar, one of his earls, defending the forecastle with Vige and a few survivors, called to the dog, "We have lost our master!"

At once Vige plunged into the sea. He swam ashore and ran howling to the summit of a hill where he remained, refusing all food, until he died.

GELERT

TRUSTY GUARDIAN

HUNTING horns sounded flourishes, dogs barked, and horses stamped in the castle courtyard, as Llewellyn, a prince of Wales, mustered his cavalcade for the chase. Before he galloped off, Llewellyn cast a glance toward the doorway where his great Irish Wolfhound, Gelert, stood sentinel. A gift--a truly royal one--from King John in 1205, the wiry-coated, greyhound-like animal was a splendid specimen of his breed, tallest of all dogs and among the strongest, able to overtake and drag down gigantic elk, standing six feet at the shoulder. The Romans had known his kind and matched them in cruel combat in the arena. Fierce though they could be, it was often said of wolfhounds:

> "And all their manners do confess
> True courage dwells in gentleness."

Gelert would not hunt today. He was left to guard his master's infant son and heir in the absence of the child's mother, nurse, and all the servants of the household. The babe slept soundly in his cradle in an inner chamber. Surely with Gelert on the watch, he would be safe.

In mid-course, Llewellyn left the chase. Without his favorite hound he had no heart for it. Besides, a nameless apprehension gripped him. Setting spurs to his steed, he rode home at full speed. Then, as a poet tells the tale :

"But when he gained the castle door,
    Aghast the chieftain stood ;
The hound was smeared with gouts of gore,
    His lips and fangs ran blood."

Frantic, Llewellyn rushed to his son's room. One glance showed him the cradle overturned, coverings drenched with the same crimson that stained the muzzle of his once-trusted hound. The furious prince drew his sword and dealt Gelert a death blow. Only then did he scan all the chamber. In one corner lay his child, alive and unharmed. Close at hand was the body of a huge, gaunt wolf, gashed and torn by Gelert's teeth. The beast had crept in and leaped for the cradle when the big Wolfhound's charge struck him.

In grieving atonement, Llewellyn built a chapel and raised a tomb for his hound

"Where never could the spearman pass,
    Or the forester, unmoved."

To this day the tale is told in Wales, and the grave known as Beth Gelert.

Paul Brown

HELP AND HOLD

A STAG OR THEIR MASTER'S HEAD

NONE but a nobleman might own a Scottish Deerhound, and no lord of Scotland was prouder of his leash of those splendid creatures than Sir William St. Claire. Their names were Help and Hold, and many an antlered stag had they brought to bay or pulled down in flight over moor or mountain crag. So huge were they that when they stood on their hind legs and placed their paws on their master's shoulders they could almost look him full in the face.

Help and Hold followed St. Claire that day he rode to hunt in the train of Robert Bruce, who had wrested his realm from the grasp of the English and been crowned King of Scotland. Nearest to the fierce joy of combat was the thrill of the chase, and today there was great sport in store. Huntsmen started a mighty white stag, vainly pursued by the King before and greatly coveted.

The royal hounds were loosed, horsemen galloping hard after them, but they could not overtake the swift quarry, though they turned him and he was not yet lost. As the Scottish chieftains reined in their blown mounts, St. Claire made his boast.

Paul Brown

Help and Hold alone, he avowed, could bring down yonder stag, and he would wager his head upon it.

The King, wrath rising in him, listened grimly. Never one to brook rivalry, he gave his stern answer.

Let the wager stand, he decreed. St. Claire must abide by his word. And against the noble's head the Bruce staked a rich portion of the royal domain: all Pentland forest, its moor and its hills.

St. Claire turned pale. How rashly had he spoken! He murmured a prayer to Christ, the Blessed Virgin, and St. Katherine, as he commanded his staghounds to be unleashed.

Baying, Help and Hold bounded forward. Gallantly they coursed the white stag. They were close on his heels when he swerved and plunged into a river. In they leaped after him, but Sir William's heart sank as he rode to the bank with the rest of the hunt. In the water, all the advantage was the stag's.

Heads just above the surface, the great hounds forged onward with powerful strokes. Well they knew that if they could not reach their prey in the river, he would escape. The stag was close to the farther shore now. At the last moment, Help spurted forward, turned him, and Hold seized him. They killed and towed him back to their master's feet. The lands wagered, conveyed to Sir William, founded his fortune. Some years later he fell in battle against the Saracens in Spain. He lies buried in Rosslyn Chapel, and at the feet of his marble effigy is sculptured as grateful token the image of a staghound.

DOG OF ST. ROCH

PESTILENCE AND A PATRON

It happened in those terrible years in the mid-fourteenth century, when the Black Death stalked through Europe. Spreading from the East over trade routes, the pestilence, a form of bubonic plague, ravaged Italy, France, and England. It claimed countless victims--some say as many as 450 millions. Against that somber background shines the story of a man's self-sacrifice and the faithfulness of his dog.

Roch was born in Montpellier in the south of France, a nephew of the governor of the city. Much of his career is misted by legend, but it seems definite that when he reached manhood, he gave his fortune to the poor, became a monk and journeyed through the countryside, ministering to the peasants. Everywhere he went he was followed by his dog.

Having made a pilgrimage to Rome, Roch was in Italy when the Black Death struck that land in 1348. Thousands fled in panic, finding no safety anywhere, stricken in their tracks. While families in wild terror deserted their own dying, Roch went from city to city, caring for the sick in the overwhelmed hospitals. Finally a telltale swelling sore broke out on one of

his thighs, and the plague's agony and sleeplessness seized him. Strength enough remained to him to totter out of the hospital where he had been toiling, so that he would not be a burden. He dragged himself to the edge of a wood and lay down to die.

There his dog found him. Whimpering, the animal licked his helpless master. Then he trotted away.

In a glade in the depths of the forest, a party of noble lords and ladies had encamped, seeking refuge from the plague. Aware that each day might be their last, they spent their time in feasting and revelry, careless of the fate of others. As they sat at a banquet, they saw a strange dog walk up to the table, seize a loaf of bread in his mouth and lope off through the trees. Day after day, the same performance took place. At last the chief of the party trailed the dog and watched him give the loaf to his dying master. Roch, an old verse quaintly declares, rendered up his soul, free of sin, and died a good Christian in the arms of his dog. It is related that the noble man was so moved that he dedicated his own life to the service of his fellow men.

Roch, sainted, became the patron of the plague-stricken and of all dogs. He is one of that company of holy men, often represented in images and paintings in company with a dog: Saints Huber, Bernard, Benignus, Wedelin, and Dominic. St. Roch's dog is shown with a loaf of bread grasped in his mouth.

MATHE

FALSE TO A KING

THE Greyhound, Mathe, was a royal dog. Such had been no few of his breed since ancient times.

Carvings depict them on the tombs of the Egyptian Pharoahs as early as 4000 B.C. And in Mathe's own land, England, Greyhounds had been prized for centuries, a law of 1066 proclaiming that "no meane person may keepe any greihounds."

Mathe was praised as beautiful beyond measure, and his owner was "no meane person" but King Richard II. All the court remarked the hound's devotion to the King. When the monarch prepared to ride forth hunting, the master of his kennels loosed Mathe, and the dog ran to caress Richard, springing up to place paws fondly on his shoulders.

The day came when rebellion stirred in the realm. Henry of Lancaster returned from exile to lead an army to victory and imprison his liege lord in a castle. Richard, still treated with courtesy, was invited one morning to ride with his conqueror.

Then before a great concourse of people, gathered before the castle, there befell a strange thing, related by Froissart in his *Chronicles*. Mathe, unleashed as usual, darted straight to

the side of Lancaster, fawning on him and showing him all the affection with which he formerly had favored Richard, whom he now ignored.

"What does this mean?" demanded the astonished Duke. "Cousin," replied the King, "it means a great deal for you and very little for me."

"How? Pray explain it."

Richard, firm believer in omens and divination, held no doubt of the widespread superstition of his time that Greyhounds possessed the power to foretell the future. His answer came sorrowfully but positively.

"I understand by it that this greyhound fondles and pays his court to you this day as King of England, which you surely will be, and I shall be deposed, for the natural instinct of the dog shows it to him. Keep him therefore by your side, for he will now leave me and follow you."

Thirty thousand, Froissart declares, witnessed the untoward behavior of the Greyhound that day. Before long Mathe proved a true prophet. Richard, dethroned in 1399, died in prison, and Lancaster wore the crown as King Henry IV.

Mathe is recorded in history as one of those rare dogs, unfaithful to a beloved master. Yet he could not act otherwise, the chronicler explains, since "he was lightened wyth the lampe of fore-knowledge."

BLACK DOG OF NEWGATE

HE HAUNTED THE GUILTY

A STRAY black dog crept into the dreadful, reeking gloom of London's Newgate Prison. He may have been looking for his master or seeking food even in that unlikely spot, for at that period in the thirteenth century England was in the grip of a frightful famine. If turnkeys saw him enter, they paid no heed. No man ever knew his true name. Yet the gaunt creature which slunk into Newgate that evening was destined to become immortal.

Chains clanked on dank stones where prisoners, fettered to the walls, strove to smother misery with sleep. Here lay brutal criminals, awaiting execution for bloody deeds, and here, too, languished poor wretches, men and women, jailed under the merciless laws of the day for no worse than a trifling theft. Many were close to starvation. Free of the fierce pangs of hunger were only those who had bought or begged food or been fed by relatives--they and a furtive group, clustered in a dark corner. And it was these last who saw the black dog.

Seeming huge, a veritable monster in the shadows, the jet animal loomed over them. His eyes gleamed with a baleful light, and his jaws slavered. The prisoners cringed and cowered away from him. Maybe this was his dog.

A short time before a new felon had been thrust into New gate, a man clad all in black, accused of sorcery, 'twas said. This crew of murderers and mutineers in the corner, famished and desperate, had fallen upon him in the dead of night and slaughtered him. Now here was his dog, his familiar spirit did not the Devil often take the form of a black dog?--come to avenge his master. While Newgate echoed to the wild shrieks of the murderers, the black dog vanished.

He came again and again, so men swore. Always he reappeared just before inmates were dragged off to be hanged. The doomed stared down from the cart carrying them through crowded streets to the gallows on Tyburn Hill to perceive the black dog, a nemesis following them to their death.

A glimpse of the black dog was enough to drive prisoners in screaming panic to rush the gates where guards cut most of them down or drove them back. Those who escaped usually were recaptured, and it was the black dog himself, they vowed, that had helped hound them.

Many released from Newgate could quote the couplet:

> "Say to the world when thou art freed from hell,
> Newgate's Black Dog thou sawest and knowest too well."

He was a more fearsome spectacle, declared those who had beheld him, than Cerberus, the three-headed dog that is the guardian of the infernal regions. "Black he was, with curling snakes for hairs, his eyes like torches; his breath was poison and smoke came from his nostrils. His tongue was a clapper tolling poor men to ring a peal in hell... and he rent them with ravening paws to tear out their bowels."

For years, for centuries, the specter of the Black Dog haunted Newgate. Perhaps other strays, like the first one which began the legend, wandered into the prison from time to time, convincing witnesses that the apparition was a horrible reality. ·

In a sense, it was real. The Black Dog was a black conscience.

TÖLPEL

GOD'S GIFT TO LUTHER

HIS name, translated from German, meant scamp or clown, and the jolly, playful dog lived up to it, nor was there any gloom or austerity in the home of his master, Martin Luther, to discourage his pranks. The grim and perilous days were past when that valiant preacher and scholar had achieved the Protestant Reformation. Family and followers lifted voices not only in Luther's majestic hymn, *A Mighty Fortress Is Our God*, but in merry folk songs as well. Halls rang with the laughter of children, playing with Tölpel. The dog did not resent it when the small daughter of the house was rough with him, and the preacher, watching, remarked: "We see now the meaning of the text, 'Ye shall rule over the beasts of the field,' for the dog bears everything from the child." Often Luther admired the agility and appetite of his pet. At dinner one day, he looked up from a slice of meat he was about to eat to see Tölpel's eyes fixed on it with hungry intensity. "Ah," he said with a smile, "if only I could pray to God as that dog is looking at this piece of meat!"

Tölpel found a place in his master's *Table Talk,* wise words uttered by the great German and recorded by his followers.

Paul Brna

One of the children had asked that question which has come to the mind of all who love dogs, "Will there be any dogs in Heaven?" Luther answered, speaking from his faith and his knowledge of a child's heart:

"Certainly there will be, for Peter calls that day the time of restitution of all things. Then, as is clearly said elsewhere, God will create new Tölpels with skin of gold and hair of pearls. There God will be in all. No animal will eat any other. Snakes and toads, and other beasts, which are poisonous on account of original sin, will then be not only harmless but even nice to play with."

Tölpel, text and companion to a famous preacher and beloved playmate of his children, led a happy life. If other dogs, neglected and mistreated, were not so fortunate, that was because dogs were so numerous they were unappreciated. On that theme, Luther delivered a brief and eloquent sermon:

"The dog is the most faithful of animals and would be much esteemed were it not so common. Our Lord God has made his greatest gifts the commonest."

POMPEY

A PUG FOR ORANGE

Pickets around the Dutch camp were drowsy and too few, and officers of the guard careless in inspecting outposts that black night in 1572. This army, come to relieve Mons from Spanish siege, was strong, but no less formidable was the investing force under the Duke of Alva, Philip II's cruel commander who had brought fire and sword to devastate the Low Countries. By their lax watch, Dutchmen were risking the life of the leader and heart of their cause, William the Silent, Prince of Orange and Count of Nassau, whose tent was pitched in the center of the encampment.

Yet there was one sentinel that was alert: the little dog curled up on the Prince's cot. Though he was slumbering as soundly as his master, his was the keen, never-dormant instinct of the good watchdog. The silvery-coated Pompey was of the breed, probably imported from China and long favored in Holland, a breed then known as camuses, meaning crooked or snubnosed. Today we call them Pugs and borrow back the name to describe people as having "a pug nose."

Down on the unwary Dutch in the small hours marched the

Paul Brown

intrepid Colonel Julian de Romero at the head of six hundred
Spanish veterans, wearing white shirts over their armor to
distinguish each other in the darkness. They slipped past the
sentries and had struck the camp before the alarm was given.
Through carnage and chaos dashed Romero with a picked
detachment--straight toward the Prince's tent. The slaughter
of William the Silent would likely bring speedy collapse to
Dutch resistance and deal a terrible blow to religious and civic
liberty, for which he stood champion.

And still the weary Prince and his guards slept profoundly.
Despite the clash of arms and shrieks of the dying, all slept on
but Pompey. The Pug leaped up, whined and barked frantically.
Yet not till he scratched his master's face could he waken him.
As William burst from his tent, onrushing Spaniards cut down
his two secretaries. By the barest of margins the Prince reached
his horse, kept ready saddled, flung himself on its back and
made his escape. The baffled raiders, perforce content with the
heavy toll they had taken in the camp, beat a retreat.

"But for my little dog I should have been killed," William
acknowledged.

Always afterward he kept Pompey and other Pugs by his
side. It is said that Pompey saved his master's life on another
occasion, but at last William fell victim to an assassin, hired
by Philip of Spain.

At the foot of statues of the Prince, both in Holland and in
the United States, is sculptured a Pug in grateful memory of
Pompey's warning on that nearly fatal night. When the great
Dutchman's great-grandson ascended the throne of England
as William III, Pugs became the vogue and were adorned with
orange ribbons in honor of the House of Orange.

MARY OF SCOTLAND'S SKYE

HE DARED THE SCAFFOLD

IT was Mary Stuart's last day on earth. She was the daughter of a King of Scotland and in line of succession to England's throne. At fifteen she had wed the King of France. Widowed, she had claimed her right as Queen of Scots and ruled till rebellion drove her into exile. Yet for all her high estate she must perish on the scaffold. She had sought refuge in England, only to be cast into prison by her bitter rival, Queen Elizabeth, who now condemned her to be beheaded. After nineteen years of confinement and despair, death was not unwelcome.

Even beyond the faithful few of her court who shared her imprisonment, dogs had been Mary's solace, along with the doves which perched on her window sill. "My only pleasure," she declared, "is in all the little dogs I can get."

A small Skye Terrier was the Queen's favorite. Surely he sensed the impending tragedy, as dogs can, when Mary knelt to say her last prayer. Perhaps he whined and tried to run and nestle close beside her in bewildered sorrow, and her ladies held him back.

Arrayed as for a festival, Mary, Queen of Scots, was led to

Paul Brown

execution. Beneath her gown of black velvet, stamped with gold, she wore a camisole and petticoat of scarlet, for before she was beheaded she would be partially disrobed, and her blood would blend with the hue of her undergarments. At the last moment, a cruel refusal to permit any of her household to accompany her was withdrawn. Two ladies-in-waiting and four men followed the doomed Queen--they and one other.

With unwavering courage, still beautiful at forty-five, Mary mounted the scaffold. Calmly she listened to Elizabeth's decree of death and, stanchly refusing to abandon her Catholic faith, she made the sign of the Cross. The headsman, black-clad and masked, knelt and begged her forgiveness and she gave it with all her heart. Then she sank to her knees before the block. No sooner had she done so than a shaggy form crept forward unnoticed. The Skye Terrier, as if he feared being driven away, swiftly hid beneath his mistress's skirts.

Down flashed the ax. Twice more the headsman, shaken or clumsy, was forced to strike before he accomplished his purpose. Thereupon assembled witnesses heard a faint cry. The Skye crawled forth from his concealment and crouched between the Queen's severed head and shoulders. He would not move until one of Mary's ladies gathered him up, covered with blood, and carried him away. Though he did not survive his mistress long but pined away, he still lives in history's pages.

TURULETTE AND SCHWARZ

THEY RAN ERRANDS

"TURULETTE, let's take a walk," invited the French philosopher, Pierre Charron.

Quickly and eagerly, the small Terrier brought her master his hat, then his gloves and cane, and the two stepped out for a promenade through the streets of Paris.

The intelligent Turulette, taught to perform various tasks, was a shining example of obedience training, as it is termed today. No hired servant could have rendered more cheerful service, nor could Charron afford one, for he was poor. His book, *Sagesse*, dealt with wisdom, and Turulette helped prove the maxim that wisdom is better than riches. She carried messages to Charron's friends, whose names and addresses she knew. A rack of printed cards hung by his door. When groceries were needed, Charron tied a card to the dog's collar, told her which shop to visit, and off she scampered; shortly a delivery boy arrived with the order. Usually the Terrier's trip included a call at the bakery with a card reading: "A biscuit for Turulette." This and her master's affection were all the reward she asked. At bedtime she fetched her master's slippers and

Paul Brown

nightcap. When Charron gave a birthday party, Turulette was despatched at the end of the repast to a cafe which promptly sent over a tray of after-dinner coffee. Afterwards she danced on her hind legs for the entertainment of the guests.

Alas, there was one maxim her master had not taught her: "Distrust is the mother of safety." Turulette was friendly to all. An evil old woman, a seller of broken glass, enticed the little dog, killed her with a bottle, skinned her and sold her hide.

Another accomplished errand dog of a later day was a black Poodle named Schwarz. His master, a professor at the German University of Heidelberg, frequently sent him to a shop across the street from his home to bring back a sack of pipe tobacco, while neighbors watched Schwarz perform admiringly, and the owner's chest puffed with pride. It so happened that the professor moved to a town one hundred and fifty miles away where a tobacconist was again located just across the street.

"Schwarz, tobacco," his owner commanded after breakfast one morning.

The dog only stood and stared at him, and the professor repeated the order. Schwarz, still not moving, whined and cringed. In a fit of anger, the professor shouted at his pet and kicked him cruelly. The Poodle licked his hand and slunk out of the door, tail between legs.

Days passed, and he did not return; surely he must have been stolen. But on the tenth day, a gaunt dog feebly crawled into the professor's room, in his mouth a bedraggled sack of tobacco with the Heidelberg shop's label. He had averaged thirty miles a day, faithfully carrying out his errand to the only tobacco store he knew. As he placed the sack in his owner's hands, Schwarz dropped dead.

FOOLE AND GALLANT

SENTRIES IN THE NEW WORLD

IN the summer of 1603, Martin Pring, master mariner, anchored his vessels, *Speedwell* and *Discoverer*, in Cape Cod Bay and sent men ashore to build a stockade. None of the crew was happier to set foot on dry land than two members, taken aboard at Bristol, England: a pair of fine, large Mastiffs named Foole and Gallant.

Paw-prints they left, as they bounded along the beach, were not the first canine ones on the soil of the New World. The Indians had dogs of their own, and as early as 1509 Spaniards had used war dogs against the tribes of the West Indies. But a boast could be made that Foole and Gallant landed seventeen years before another Mastiff and a Spaniel, which came over on the *Mayflower*.

Indians of these shores gave the English friendly greeting and watched them cut and load their ships with sassafras bark, high in value since it was used as a sovereign remedy against many maladies. The red folk delighted to dance and sing to the tune of a sailor's guitar. Whenever they overstayed their welcome, Martin Pring had only to loose the "great and fearful Mastives," whereupon the Indians fled with outcries of terror.

Of Foole they stood in particular dread. He had been taught to carry a half-pike in his mouth, and no doubt the Indians believed him capable of wielding it. Both the Mastiffs served as

escorts; one of them brought safely back to camp an adventurer who had wandered six miles from his companions.

After the *Discoverer* had been laden and sailed for England, the temper of the Indians suddenly turned hostile. Seven score of them, armed with bows and arrows, surrounded the stockade and tried to persuade the four musketeers posted there to open the gate. Instead the guard signaled the *Speedwell*, and she fired a warning gun.

The shot woke a working party, asleep in the forest during the noon-day heat. The Englishmen whistled up the two dogs but did not stir until a second alarm convinced them the situation was serious. Then, snatching up arms, they marched for the shore. Gallant and Foole, the latter with a half-pike in his jaws, strode along as the rearguard.

Red warriors had closed in on the greatly outnumbered working party before they caught sight of the huge dogs. "More afraid of them than twentie of our men," Martin Pring wrote, the Indians pretended that they were only acting in jest and slipped away. Yet later they set the woods afire in an attempt to burn out the invaders. They failed and the *Speedwell*, cargo and crew safely aboard, set sail for home.

Perhaps merchants of Bristol rewarded the big dogs, which had saved part of their venture, with haunches of beef and ornamented collars. Martin Pring does not say, but in the log of his voyages he took pains to inscribe gratefully the names and deeds of Foole and Gallant. And not many years later William Shakespeare in Henry V would write of such as they: "England breeds very valiant creatures; their mastiffs are of unmatchable courage."

BUNGEY

AT QUEEN ELIZABETH'S COURT

BUNGEY—he looks from his portrait to have been part large Spaniel and part Setter—was as accomplished a courtier as his master, Sir John Harington. Sir John, whether he was writing love poems, epigrams, or about sanitation, was apt to be so outspoken that his god mother, Queen Elizabeth, scolded him. But Bungey, also a favorite with ladies of the court, was more discreet. The dog carried messages as far as one hundred miles, "nor was it ever tolde our ladie Queene," his master acknowledged, "that this Messenger did ever blab ought concerninge his highe trust, as others have done in more special matters."

Once when Bungey was delivering two bottles of sack wine in a cordage carrier, its strings broke. The dog hid one bottle in the rushes and went on with the second in his mouth. Two thirsty fellows, who had witnessed the whole procedure, waited curiously to see what would happen. Just as they were about to help themselves to the hidden bottle, Bungey returned, whisked it from under their hands and took it on to its destination.

Bones, Sir John observed, were Bungey's only pay, nor were

they ever bones of contention. The dog more than earned his keep as a companion and messenger, as Harington confessed in an epigram praising him:

> "He only fed my pleasure, not my purse.
> Yet that same Dogge, I may say this and boast it,
> Hath found my purse with gold when I have lost it."

Captured by two duck hunters, Bungey was presented by them to the Spanish Ambassador. Being the courtier dog he was, he so ingratiated himself that the envoy would not admit Sir John's claim when he finally located his pet. The English man proved his ownership by ordering the dog to bring him a roasted pheasant from the Spaniard's dinner table. The Spaniel-Setter's quick obedience showed that he would retrieve birds under any circumstances.

Bungey, accompanying Harington on a horseback ride one day, several times leaped as high as the horse's neck in attempts to caress his beloved master. Sir John was puzzled by the dog's sudden demonstration of affection, until he saw him creep into a thicket to lie down and die. The Knight realized then that Bungey had sensed his end was near and was bidding him farewell.

But Bungey still lives in literature. Harington caused his portrait to be engraven on the frontispiece of his translation of *Orlando Furioso*, where the dog stands chained to a marble portal, vigilant to admit only friendly readers.

BOY

ACCUSED OF WITCHCRAFT

BOY was a white Poodle and adroit at performing tricks like most of his breed. He would spring up on a table beside his master, Prince Rupert, and act as if he were whispering in his ear. He trotted around with a monkey seated like a jockey on his back. In the presence of King Charles I, who loved dogs, he sat up respectfully. Whenever anyone mentioned Parliament, hostile to his master and the King, Boy barked angrily.

During the bitter strife and civil war, destined to cost Charles his throne and his head, Boy became the best-known dog in England. Because he was a favorite of the King and the pet of Rupert, the dashing leader of Royalist cavalry, the Poodle attracted the attention of their enemies. Those tricks he did so well furnished an opportunity to Roundhead pamphleteers and cartoonists. They accused Boy of witchcraft, and in a day when men and women were tried and executed as witches, it was easy to make people believe that an unusually clever dog was a familiar of the devil. Widely distributed broadsides declared Boy was really a handsome Lapland woman, changed into a dog--that he could nose out hidden treasure-that he could make himself invisible, and Prince Rupert as well--that he was weapon-proof--that he attended church and all but took down the sermon in shorthand for his own evil ends--that he possessed the gift of tongues and conversed with his master in a language that sounded like Hebrew.

A cartoon pictured Boy and a Cromwellian dog named Pepper being set on to fight, with backers shouting: "To him, Pudel!" and "Bite him, Peper!" The dogs were shown defying each other with speeches in "balloons" reading: "Round head curr!" "Cavalier's dog!" Another cartoon affirmed that Boy was "whelped by a malignant water-witch."

Whether Boy was sorcerer enough to take note of the silly but vicious attacks is not stated, nor is their effect on his master, yet no man likes to see his dog abused. In any event, Prince Rupert continued to take his devoted companion along on all his campaigns. Always he ordered the Poodle tied to a wagon wheel in the rear when he and his squadrons galloped into action.

But at the battlefield of Marston Moor in 1644, Rupert forgot to give the usual order for his dog's safety. Boy, left unleashed, followed the Prince into the thick of the fray. The dog never found his master in the confusion, for the day went disastrously for the Cavaliers. Their ranks were broken by a cavalry charge, led by Oliver Cromwell. Grim Roundhead infantry, chanting a psalm as they marched into battle, drove the Royalists before them. The routed troops of the King surrendered or fled. Rupert, fleeing for his life, never witnessed the fate of the dog which had been searching everywhere for him. A Roundhead soldier caught sight of the white Poodle, leveled his matchlock and fired. Boy fell dead. Only because the soldier was skilled

Paul Brown

in necromancy himself, as his party ex-plained, had he been able to slay the invulnerable witch-dog.

Triumphant Roundheads gloated over Boy's death.

"Sad Cavaliers' Rupert invites you all
That does survive, to his Dog's Funerall.
Close-mourners are the witch, Pope, & Devill.
That much lament yo'r late befallen evill."

LE DIABLE

SMUGGLER IN DISGUISE

CUSTOMS guards along the border began seeing something white gleam faintly in the moonlight. Before they could raise their muskets and fire, it disappeared in the black shadows of the underbrush, and all pursuit was futile. Perhaps smugglers were using children again, fleet boys and girls, hard to spot and harder still to catch. Smugglers stopped at nothing to slip goods across without paying duty, risking death from a bullet or long years in a dank, rat-infested jail. There was plenty of money in "the trade," especially in lace smuggled from Belgium to sell at bargain prices in France, and a great deal of contraband was being run through during the eighteenth century.

Guards were reinforced and redoubled their vigilance. It was some time before they discovered that smugglers were using dogs--big, strong animals, able to carry high-paying loads of such light-weight articles as lace and cigars. Dogs were sent out not only singly but in packs. The leader of one of the most successful canine smuggling bands was a large, whitish mongrel called Le Diable--The Devil.

Border patrols kept a sharp lookout for him, but he always

Paul Brown

saw them first. Like many another smuggler's dog, his training had included beatings by men dressed as Customs officials,
and he gave a wide berth to anybody in such uniforms. It was
no help when orders warned the posts to watch particularly
for a white dog. Le Diable's master frequently disguised him
by dyeing his hide brown, black or gray.

Scouting ahead, Le Diable never failed to scent an ambush
of border guards and skirt it with his pack or turn back when
the cordon was drawn too close. If the dogs crept past the line
safely, the leader entered the house of the receiver of smuggled
goods alone, while his followers waited in concealment and
emerged only when Le Diable's bark signaled all clear.

According to a Customs estimate, more than 55,000 pas-
sages of the Rhine frontier alone were made by dogs, carrying an aggregate of many tons of contraband merchandise.
So little luck in catching them did the authorities have that
they resorted to keeping an eye on dog owners living along
the border. Any one who showed signs of sudden wealth was
investigated on the theory—often enough correct—that he had
grown rich from the trips of his smuggling dogs. It was only
when the guards started employing dogs of their own that the
traffic was largely stopped.

Le Diable had smuggled 50,000 francs' worth of lace, along
with other goods, before his career came to an end. One night
a sharpshooter at a Customs post sighted him swimming a
river and fired. His bullet carried true, and the dog sank, the
waters closing over him.

MARQUISE AND BOUNCE

A SHARP PEN AND BODYGUARDS

A DARK figure glided into the bedroom of Alexander Pope at midnight. Moonlight glinted on the knife in his hand. The intruder, Pope's valet, moved silently, knowing the location of every piece of furniture, and the noted English author slumbered on soundly. Even if he waked and struggled, his weak, deformed body could offer little resistance to the would-be murderer.

Pope's savage satires had made him many bitter enemies. Perhaps some of them had hired this assassin, or the man's motive may have been robbery, since he knew his employer's writings had earned a fortune. Before he could strike, glass crashed and the poet's Poodle, Marquise, burst through a French window and flew at the valet's throat. The fellow was badly mauled when other servants, brought by Pope's outcries, pulled the dog off.

Nerves severely shaken, Pope resolved never to be without a canine bodyguard. When the brave Poodle died, the writer played doubly safe by choosing a magnificent Great Dane. Bounce was so powerful a monster that even in playfulness he overturned guests, but to his misshapen master he was all gentleness and devotion. Pope had no need of the pistols he carried on his walks through the grounds of his villa at Twick-

enham—not with Bounce stalking along by his side. Angry hatreds were aroused by Pope's vitriolic book, The Dunciad, yet its victims only fumed and sputtered from afar. Nobody was rash enough to venture bodily violence against a man whose constant companion and guardian was a Great Dane.

"My only friend," Pope called Bounce, but that was poetic exaggeration. The author rejoiced in comrades and admirers of his genius who were also fond of his dog. Jonathan Swift wrote a tribute, "Bounce to Fop—An Epistle from a Dog at Twickenham to a Dog at Court," in which Bounce was made to boast:

> "Nobles whom arms or arts adorn
> Wait for my infants yet unborn.
> None but a peer of wit and grace
> Can hope a puppy of my race."

The Prince of Wales was one of the fortunate ones, favored with an offspring of Bounce's. The gift arrived wearing a collar with an inscription, barbed by Pope's irony:

> "I am His Highness' dog at Kew.
> Pray tell me, sir, whose dog are you?"

Bounce died during an absence from home of his master. Sadly Pope wrote: "I dread to inquire into the particulars of the fate of Bounce. Perhaps you concealed them, as Heaven often does unhappy events, in pity to the survivors, or not to hasten on my end by sorrow. I doubt not how much Bounce was lamented."

The world must hold Bounce and Marquise in grateful memory. They protected one whose pen, sharp though it often was, flowed also with wisdom and grace and left a priceless legacy to English literature.

GENGISK

A MONARCH'S GREAT DANE

Loping through the dusk, the huge hound easily kept pace with the horse of his master, Frederick the Great. Gengisk, the Great Dane, was not supposed to be following the solitary rider this evening; he had been shut in a tent but had broken free. So it happened that the King of Prussia, rash to ride alone through country where parties of the enemy might at any time be encountered, gained an unexpected escort.

Abruptly Gengisk began to show signs of excitement. He leaped up to tug at his master's boot, and when Frederick paid him no heed, sprang higher in an attempt to seize the reins. The monarch then halted, listened where the hound pointed and heard the distant pounding of hoofs. Hastily he dismounted and led his steed beneath a culvert. Hardly had he hidden, when a troop of Cossacks galloped across the bridge above him. Frederick, holding Gengisk's muzzle to muffle his growls, released it after the foe had passed to pat his savior gratefully.

Gengisk fought at the King's side through wars with Austria and was several times wounded. At the Battle of Soor, the Great Dane was captured with the imperial baggage and presented by

Paul Brown

an enemy general to his wife. After Prussia's victory, a special clause in the peace treaty demanded Gengisk's restoration. In an affecting reunion, the stern ruler threw his arms around the big animal's neck and wept. "The more I see of men," Frederick declared, "the better I like my dog."

Meanwhile the King had acquired a Terrier to fill the gap made by his favorite's absence, and the small dog jealously resented the rival he regarded as an intruder. For days the Great Dane treated the Terrier's yapping and snapping with dignified forbearance. At last he picked up the little upstart by the nape of his neck, swam the Danube, then in flood, with him, marooned him on the farther bank and swam home.

When Gengisk, weakened by wounds and battle fatigue, died, he was buried beneath a granite monument in the rose garden of Frederick's palace, Sans Souci.

PAUL REVERE'S DOG

HE HELPED SPEED THE RIDE

HIS dog followed him when he left his house on Boston's North Square that fateful night of the 18th of April, 1775. Doubtless Paul Revere told him to go home, since he was setting out, "Ready to ride and spread the alarm Through every Middlesex village and farm."

Like countless other dogs on innumerable other occasions, the dog looked hurt, turned back, then trotted after his master again. It was far too risky to shout "Go home!" with sentries on patrol and British Regulars on the march to Lexington to capture John Hancock, Sam Adams, and the Americans' military stores at Lexington and Concord. Revere gave up and let his pet come along, and fortunate it was that he did.

Paul met the two men who were to row him across the Charles River, where a British frigate lay on guard. It was then he realized he had forgotten cloth to muffle the oars. One of the patriots knew a girl who lived in the neighborhood. He whistled softly beneath her window, and when she looked out whispered up urgently. Down fluttered a flannel petticoat, still warm. But now it came to Revere that in his haste he had for-

Paul Brown

gotten another important item. He was not "ready to ride"—he had left his spurs at his house.

Scribbling a note to his wife Rachel, he bent down, tied it to his dog's collar and gave him an order. Now the dog did go home, racing off through the dark streets. Soon the trusty animal returned carrying the spurs, and his master hastened on,

"Booted and spurred, with a heavy stride."

At the river a farewell pat, a command to be quiet. We can imagine the dog sitting disconsolately on the shore, whimpering a little. A landing, and Paul Revere swung into the saddle of Mr. Larkin's swift horse and galloped off.

Near Charlestown two British officers approached to halt the express rider. One rode down on him, the other circled to head him off. Revere whirled his steed. Surely those spurs were useful then. Cross-country he sped, the Britishers quickly out distanced, one of them bogged down. On Revere dashed, alarming houses along his route. Only after he had brought his warning to Lexington and was riding on to Concord did the British capture him and take his horse. By then his memorable errand had been done.

So a dog must be honored, too, for that historic ride. When Paul Revere told the story of his exploit to his children, always a favorite part was how his dog had brought him his forgotten spurs.

SIRRAH

A SHEPHERD'S COLLIE

LIFE brightened for the black Collie, thin and woebegone, when a dour drover sold him to the owner of Ettrick Farm. Sirrah was given to the farmer's son, James Hogg, just sixteen and ready after apprenticeship as a cowherd to take the responsibility of a flock of sheep.

Sirrah grew to love the cheerful lad, who fed and trained him so kindly and thoroughly. James was always singing lays of old Scottish minstrels, taught him by his mother. Soon the young shepherd began to compose charming songs of his own while he pastured his sheep, marshaled and guarded by his Collie, in the heather of the Ettrick Hills. There was singing, too, at home on the Sabbath, with the voices of the family lifted in psalms. Sirrah, fond of music, lifted his head and joined in at the top of his lungs. Banished from the shocked gathering and shut up in the byre, he still could be heard chiming in with praises of the Lord.

One pitch-black night in the hills, there was no thought of song. James and another youthful shepherd, in charge with their dogs of a large flock of seven hundred lambs, were worried. It

Paul Brown

was weaning time and hard to keep track of so many restless, bleating creatures, even though they were separated into three groups. James, groping through the darkness on his rounds, lost all trace of them. All three divisions had scampered off and vanished. The shepherd shouted desperately to his dog:

"Sirrah, my man! They're awa'!"

Instantly Sirrah plunged off in pursuit. James, his comrade, and the second Collie searched all night through the hills. At dawn those three met in bitter failure. Neither the lambs nor Sirrah could be found. The shepherds trudged toward home to confess the disgrace of their loss.

Suddenly the other dog barked in joy. Yonder in a glen moved a woolly mass, gathered and vigilantly kept penned there by Sirrah. Not a single one of the seven hundred was missing.

Other noted feats were performed by Sirrah until long and faithful service brought him to old age. James by then had trained a son of Sirrah's. He turned over the old dog to another shepherd whose work was lighter. Times were hard, and James Hogg felt he could not afford to keep two dogs.

"Jamie the Poeter" they were calling him now, and Scotland was singing the sweet songs he made. He would go on to join the literary great and become a friend of Scott, Wordsworth, and Byron. Fame was his, but the abandonment of his trusting companion of years must always have lain on his conscience.

Sirrah after a time refused to work for the other shepherd, though he was a good master, and he was too proud to return to his former home. But to one weakness he did yield--glimpses now and then for the brief remainder of his life, glimpses of the man he still loved. James, walking along a certain road, would sight a black Collie waiting for him. For a moment Sirrah would lay his head in his old master's hand, then turn and trot away.

SNOWBALL

ENGLAND'S GREATEST GREYHOUND

WHILE eager spectators watched, three lithe Greyhounds started a hare on the Flexton Brow course. It was likely to be an exciting run, since the course included a broad, open meadow atop a steep hill, rising to the village.

One hound was only a twelve-month-old youngster, but the other two were the celebrated Snowball and a sister of his, descended from the Great Czarina, which won forty-seven matches straight and would not leave off coursing to breed till she was thirteen.

Up the hill dashed the hare, the Greyhounds in hot pursuit, now they had their view. They ran by sight, these "gazehounds," depending not at all on their inferior powers of scent. Their quarry circled the wold and sped down the slope, doubled, ran up again. Now the winded puppy abandoned the chase. Forty times and more Snowball and his sister turned the hare but could not catch it. At length the bitch gave up, and Snowball coursed alone. After a run of more than four miles, with two ascents of the mile-high hill, he seized and killed the hare in the village. It was one of the greatest runs in sporting history.

Paul Brown

Snowball's coat was a beautiful, sleek jet black. It was his reputation that matched his name, rolling up larger and larger like a snowball. His letter and colors triumphed for the Swaffham Coursing Society. In 1799 he beat the champion of Scotland, with his backers winning heavily. Only hounds of his own blood could rival him. He won ten large silver plates and upwards of forty matches against the fastest in the field. Challenging the world, he found no takers. Bitches from all over Great Britain were brought to be bred to him at a fee of three guineas, and his progeny were worthy of him.

No less than Sir Walter Scott praised a run the hound made in his old age.

> 'Twas when fleet Snowball's head was waxen grey,
> A luckless lev'ret met him on his way.
> Who knows not Snowball? He whose race renowned
> Is still victorious on each coursing ground;
> Swaffham, Newmarket, and the Roman camp,
> Have seen them victors o'er each meaner stamp.
> In vain the youngling sought with doubling wile
> The hedge, the hill, the thicket, or the stile;
> Experience sage the lack of speed supplied,
> And in the gap he sought, the victim died.

The black Greyhound's memory is cherished today. After two centuries of English coursing, Snowball still is rated the most perfect Greyhound ever produced.

MOUSTACHE

HE CAUGHT A SPY

DRUMS rolled and the trumpets sounded a flourish. The band struck up, and through the streets of Caen, France, marched a regiment of Grenadiers.

A cross-bred Poodle watched from the curb. Born in 1799, he was still a puppy and no more than the small boys of the town could he resist the stirring summons of martial music and bright-hued uniforms. Tail wagging, he joined the parade. Though his master, a grocer, was kind, the dog followed the tall soldiers on through town. The regiment had a new recruit.

They clipped him *à la militaire* and gave the barber orders to shave and comb him once a week. His black hair jutted out from both sides of his muzzle, for all the world like the ferocious moustaches of his fellow Grenadiers, so moustache became his name. Wearing a collar identifying him as a member of the regiment, he learned to carry, to sit up at attention, to march in time and stand guard.

Soldiers love the companionship of dogs, and no regulation forbade Moustache's presence in the field. Napoleon himself in 1798 had suggested sentry dogs to his general commanding the garrison in Alexandria, Egypt, writing: "They ought to have at Alexandria a large number of dogs, which you can easily make use of by fastening them a short distance from your walls." Moustache proved that he, too, could be an alert sentinel during the Italian campaign, when his warning barks gave his regiment time to spring to arms and repulse a surprise attack by the Austrians. He took a bayonet wound in the fight.

At the Battle of Marengo, a courier galloped into the French lines. Delivering his message, the man walked freely about, observing the disposition of troops, until he met Moustache. The Poodle bristled, growled and bared his fangs. If not held back, he would have savagely attacked this soldier in French uniform. Suspicious Grenadiers searched the courier and found evidence he was an Austrian spy.

During hot, hand-to-hand fighting at Austerlitz, a young ensign of Chasseurs was mortally wounded while carrying the colors. As he fell, he ripped the flag from its staff to save it from capture by advancing enemy. He was too late--Austrian infantry had seen him and were moving up on the double. Suddenly the dying man felt a tug at his side. Moustache seized the colors in his teeth, unwound them and, dodging lunges of enemy bayonets, raced back to the French lines. For that feat, Marshall Lannes personally decorated the dog with a medal for gallantry in action, and his name was inscribed on the rolls for rations and pay.

The Chasseurs now claimed him, and he served with them until an officer, failing to recognize him, struck him with the flat of his saber. Indignantly Moustache transferred to the Dragoons. Campaigning in Spain, he was killed by a cannon ball at the taking of Badajos and buried on the field under a stone marked, "Here lies the brave Moustache." Spaniards later

Paul
Brown

broke the stone. When the Spanish Inquisition in its rancor ordered his bones dug up and burned, history listed one more tribute to the valiant French war dog.

BOATSWAIN

BYRON'S NEWFOUNDLAND

THE powerful black-and-white dog stared at his unpredictable master. That darkly handsome young Englishman was running toward the lake, limping a little on the twisted feet with which he was born. Fully dressed, he flung himself into the water. He floundered about, gasping choked cries for help. It was a convincing performance to any one who did not know that the supposedly drowning man was the poet, George Gordon Byron, an expert swimmer who would one day, like Leander, swim the Hellespont.

The dog did not hesitate. Boatswain was a Newfoundland, and rescuing the drowning was a duty bred in his every fiber. Plunging into the lake, he swam out, seized his master by his coat and towed him ashore. Byron was delighted. It was a dramatic spectacle, and the poet loved and lived drama and wrote it. He repeated the drowning trick from time to time. Boatswain, whether or not he sensed it was all acting, always played his part perfectly.

Too soon comedy gave way to tragedy. Byron was not granted even the average companionship of a decade or two which a

Paul Brown

dog's normal life span affords. Boatswain caught rabies. All through the fatal illness, the poet tenderly nursed the New-foundland, risking his life to sponge the froth from the suffer-ing creature's jaws. Boatswain injured neither him nor anyone else; in his fits of madness he bit only himself. To his death he responded with grateful affection to his master's care.

In the former monastery, Newstead Abbey, which was Byron's country seat, he ordered a vault built for his dog within the ruined chapel where the altar once stood and he gave instructions that he also was to be buried there. Upon a side of a finely sculptured pedestal was inscribed that celebrated epitaph, written by the poet.

NEAR this spot
Are deposited the remains of one
Who possessed Beauty with Vanity
Strength without Insolence
Courage without Ferocity
And all the Virtues of Man without his Vices.
This praise which would be unmeaning Flattery
If inscribed over human ashes
Is but a just tribute to the Memory of
BOATSWAIN, a Dog
Who was born at Newfoundland, May 1803,
And died at Newstead Abbey, November 18, 1808.

Byron died of malaria in Greece, where he had gone to help that country fight for its independence from Turkey. Among his possessions was found a treasured keepsake--the collar Boatswain had worn.

BARRY

ST. BERNARD TO THE RESCUE

CLOUDS cluster about the lofty Alpine peak where stands the hospice founded by St. Bernard of Menthon in the year 980 for the sake of travelers venturing through the perilous pass between Switzerland and Italy. There, about 1800, Barry was whelped.

Dignity mantled him even in puppyhood. Power was his birthright, since he was descended from the huge Molossian hounds which centuries ago marched with the invading Roman armies into Helvetia. And in Barry breathed a great share of the spirit of good will toward men that dwells in all dogs. For he was of the breed later called St. Bernards, and his mission in life was the rescue of helpless humans perishing in the deep snows.

When Barry as a puppy was sent out his first winter to begin his training, the good Augustinian monks of the hospice noted he learned more quickly than any dog they had known. His teachers were older members of the pack. Following them in patrols, he performed his duties more by instinct than imitation. Unerringly, he nosed out dummy figures, buried by the

Paul Brown

monks under drifts, and performed his practice rescues. The time came when Barry, his growth gained and his weight over 150 pounds, was ordered out with three veterans on a real search. The monks fastened his broad, spiked collar, defense against wolves, and strapped on the harness carrying a small key containing stimulant to revive freezing persons. The four big dogs plunged out into a blinding snowstorm.

That bitter cold day, as on many others in the pass, the Great White Death walked abroad. An unfortunate traveler, caught in the sudden blizzard, had sunk down exhausted in the snow. Buried under the falling flakes, he had fallen into the fatal sleep which ends in death, when Barry and his companions found him. They dug him out, and two of the dogs lay down beside him, warming him with their bodies. A third licked his face to restore him to consciousness and offer the revivifying fluid in his keg. The fourth dog trotted back to bring the monks. By this marvelous teamwork, another life was added to the long list of rescued, which today numbers more than 2500.

In ten years, Barry, in company or alone, rescued forty people. Once he trailed a little girl, lost in a storm. Gently rousing her, he persuaded her to climb on his sturdy back where she lashed herself fast. Then Barry carefully carried her back to the hospice. So celebrated did he become that the Swiss named all his breed "Barry hounds." At the age of ten, when many of his kind died, worn out by their exertions, he still carried on.

Two tales are told of his end. One declares that an avalanche- -usually the dogs could sense their coming and dodge—caught him unawares and killed him. Another relates that Barry on his forty-first rescue discovered a freezing soldier. Suddenly awakened, the trooper stared up at an animal he took for a wolf, seized his gun and shot his rescuer. Either of these fates may have happened to other Barrys. A peaceful death was the lot of the original.

Barry, retired and pensioned, spent his declining years in the pleasant town of Berne. When his health gave way, he was painlessly put to death in 1814. His mounted form is an exhibit in Berne's natural history museum.

Now travelers need no longer dare the perilous pass but speed beneath the Alps through a railroad tunnel. Yet the skier or mountaineer in distress, or the aviator who crashes near the hospice of St. Bernard, can still depend upon the blessed reassurance of old. The good monks and their saintly dogs will not fail them.

BRUTUS

ARTIST'S MODEL

IT was a beautiful drawing that young Edwin Landseer made of the grizzled old Fox Terrier, Brutus. So pleased was the dog's owner, he presented a pup of Brutus's, named after his sire, to the boy artist, then at the outset of his career as one of the foremost portrayers of animals. Soon Landseer began to draw the puppy, too, with that insight and sympathy which make one believe he could read the thoughts of dogs.

Old Brutus, it is easy to imagine, may have given this advice to his son: "Young fellow, two callings lie open to you. You may strive to become like me the most renowned rat-catcher in England—probably in the world. Or you may loaf around the studio and let Master Landseer draw pictures of you. Personally, I recommend rats. They're more fun."

Brutus II, though no rat could approach him with impunity, chose to continue as an artist's model. Always to be with the yellow-haired lad was a delight, for no one ever had greater love and understanding of dogs. In 1817 when Landseer was only fifteen—he had begun to draw when he was six—his portraits of both Brutuses were exhibited at the Royal Academy. Gallery visitors admired the head of Old Brutus, wise and venerable, and the knowing, perky expression of his lively off spring.

The young Terrier's hide was white and smooth, his small ears V-shaped, his tail docked short, and his temper with strangers even shorter. His mischievousness and belligerence made him all the better a model. Landseer's paintings usually told a story, and the escapades of Brutus often supplied it. He is the central figure in "The Larder Invaded," which won a prize of £150. In another picture, Brutus is shown challenging a Bulldog to dare enter a stable stall he has claimed as his territory. However, when his master paid a visit to paint Sir Walter Scott's huge and stately staghound, Maida, Brutus prudently remembered his manners as a guest.

Brutus had to share the limelight with other models. Under Landseer's brush and pencil, creatures came to life on canvas and paper—lions and tigers, cats and monkeys, donkeys and mules. Out hunting, the artist would drop his gun for a pad to sketch an antlered stag. Queen Victoria and lords and ladies of the court sat for him. But it was dogs he was fondest of painting, and his pictures of them brought wealth, a knighthood, and lasting fame. And Brutus held his place as his master's favorite model.

"If anything could justify a man's wish to be a dog," someone said, "it would be that Sir Edwin might paint him." Plainly Brutus rejoiced in the attention and companionship, which were his rewards for posing. Perhaps he recognized himself in his master's paintings, as dogs do their image in a mirror, once they learn it is not the reflection of some impudent interloper.

When time at last took Brutus, Landseer mourned him so deeply that, while a whole troop of dogs followed him for

BRUTUS

the rest of his life, none ever replaced the Fox Terrier in his affections.

Brutus, one feels, would have understood the artist's reply when Queen Victoria asked him how he was able so faithfully to represent the individual character of dogs in his paintings.

"By peeping into their hearts, ma'am."

MAIDA

SIR WALTER SCOTT'S STAGHOUND

ON the hearth rug in Sir Walter Scott's study, the great Scottish Deerhound Maida lay couched, listening to the familiar scratching of his master's quill pen. Chapter II of *Woodstock*, one of the long and immensely popular series of the Waverley novels, swiftly took form, with blades clashing as a Roundhead soldier struck the sword from the hand of the old cavalier, Sir Henry Lee. Scott's pen, darting on, wrote, "At this moment—"

Those words were the entrance cue for Maida into the book. Perhaps the staghound sensed, with that strange awareness of dogs, that he was occupying his master's thoughts. Scott wrote on. "—another auxiliary rushed out of the thicket to the knight's assistance. It was a large wolf-dog, in strength a mastiff, in form and almost in fleetness a greyhound. Bevis was the noblest of the kind which ever pulled down a stag, tawny-coloured like a lion, with a black muzzle and black feet with a line of white round the toes."

Thus Maida, serving as the model for *Bevis*, became one of the famous dogs of literature and helped his ailing master in his gallant and successful fight to pay off heavy debts, assumed

when his publisher failed. *Woodstock,* the first novel written after the crash, earned £8000, and Maida as Bevis, performing deeds of derring-do, appears in thirteen chapters. The staghound, a gift from Macdonnell of Glengarry, was named by Scott from a battle in which the chieftain who presented him had fought with distinguished valor. Maida shared the love of his master with a pack of greyhounds and terriers and devotedly responded to it like all the animals of Abbotsford, ranging from horses, donkeys, and hens to a small black pig. Neither Maida nor any of the succession of dogs, which filled Scott's life, his tales and poems, could bear to be long away from him. He talked often to them and believed they understood a great deal he said. Maida guarded him at night and dined from a plate at his table. In the study, at a word or a snap of Scott's fingers, the staghound would rise, stalk over to his idol and lay his head on the laird's lap for a caress. When the hound wished to leave, he thumped on the door with a huge forepaw.

The undisputed ruler of the pack, Maida asserted his authority only when the others became impudent. But the big staghound submitted in turn to an ancient and tyrannical tom cat which, Scott declared, "keeps him in the best possible order and insists on all rights of precedence and scratches with impunity the nose of an animal who would make no bones of a wolf and pull down a red deer without fear or difficulty."

Visitors greatly admired Maida's dignity and gravity. Landseer, noted portrayer of animals, painted his portrait. So many other artists followed suit that the first glimpse of a man setting up an easel and grasping a brush caused the staghound to howl and run away. Yet his likeness in engravings, on the image trays of Italian peddlers, and on German snuff-boxes, inscribed "The beloved hound of Walter Scott," made him one of the best-known dogs in the world.

When the noble Deerhound aged so that he could no longer follow his master far from the house, Scott wrote of him to a friend: "I have sometimes thought of the final cause of dogs having such short lives; for if we suffer so much in losing a dog after an acquaintance of ten or twelve years, what would it be if they were to live double that time?"

In 18241 Maida, old and feeble, died quietly on his straw bed. The staghound's grave is marked by his statue, bearing a Latin inscription translated by Sir Walter:

"Beneath the sculptured form which late you wore,
Sleep soundly, Maida, at your master's door."

FLUSH

PET OF A POET

IT was not easy for the brown, white breasted Cocker Spaniel to give up the bright meadows where he joyously hunted partridges and rabbits to be shut up in a gloomy London mansion, the pet of a sick lady who seldom rose from her couch. But Flush's hazel eyes gazed up into the invalid's pale, lovely face, framed in black ringlets, and his young heart went out to his new mistress, Elizabeth Barrett, the poet, and before long she could write, "He loves me better than the sunlight without."

Flush gave her devoted companionship and that ready, warm sympathy dogs bestow when they sense sadness in beings they adore. And cherishing him for it, Elizabeth enshrined him in verse.

> "And if one or two quick tears
>   Dropped upon his glossy ears,
>   Or a sigh came double—
>   Up he sprang in eager haste,
>   Fawning, fondling, breathing fast,
>   In a tender trouble."

Like other lovers, Flush was jealous. He growled at that dog he saw in the mirror in his mistress's room. One day a tall, handsome man came to call--the poet Robert Browning, who had written Elizabeth of his admiration of her poetry. Flush, utterly ignored, stood all the neglect he could, then nipped the intruder's leg. His mistress, scolding him, boxing his ears and refusing to speak to him after the caller left, finally told him he could come and say he was sorry. "He dashed across the room, trembling all over," Elizabeth wrote Browning, "kissed first one of my hands and then the other, and put up his paws to be shaken, and looked into my face with such beseeching eyes that you would certainly have forgiven him just as I did." Although the Spaniel again attacked his rival on his next call, Browning, who understood dogs, soon succeeded in making friends with him.

Tragedy loomed when an organized gang of dog-stealers spirited Flush away. Elizabeth was distraught, believing the threat that dog-owners, who refused the gang's demands for money, received the severed head and paws of their pet in a parcel. Hastily she furnished ransom for Flush's return. Twice more the gang, regarding Flush as a steady source of income, kidnapped him. Elizabeth's father and brothers refused to negotiate and, joined even by Browning, insisted the police be called in. But Miss Barrett would not hear of risking her pet's life. On one of the occasions, the courageous girl, accompanied only by her trembling but loyal maid, ventured into the very den of the thieves in the slums to rescue her dog and pay the sum demanded. For Flush's sake no peril was too great.

Nor was Flush forgotten in the great crisis of his mistress's life. When Elizabeth's tyrannical father denied his consent to her marriage, she and Browning eloped to Italy. "With them went the Spaniel, escaping the vengeance of old Mr. Barrett,

Paul Brown

who had ordered him killed. A member of the happy household established in Florence, Flush freely and joyfully ranged the sunlit streets and hillsides. Only two passing clouds appeared on his horizon. Jealousy seized him briefly again when a baby was born to his mistress, and once he was tormented by lusty Italian fleas until Browning rid him of the pests by clipping his curly coat.

Flush died in his old age and was buried in the courtyard, but his memory is forever green in the poems and letters he inspired. In recent years his biography was written by Virginia Woolf, and a successful play, *The Barretts of Wimpole Street*, appeared with Katharine Cornell starring as *Elizabeth* and a Spaniel playing *Flush* with all the fervor of the original.

KEEPER

EMILY BRONTË'S BOXER

NEVER strike him or he will fly at your throat!"
Such was the warning with which the big, tawny dog was given Emily Brontë, and he looked fully capable of murderous assault, if provoked. Part mastiff, part bulldog, Keeper was of the breed known today as Boxers. "His growl is more terrible than the bark, menacing as muted thunder," wrote his new mistress. Yet the gentle, fragile girl instantly took the grim, fierce creature to her heart, for she loved all animals, and a wild strain in them always appealed to her.

Keeper responded to her affection. For the rest of the world he cared nothing, but Emily was his idol. He strode at her heels in long walks across the moors and lay beside her on the rug when she read, her arm around his neck. At her command he would roar like a lion. She salved his wounds from fights with other dogs and mentioned him fondly in her letters. She painted his portrait in water-colors. Although Keeper does not appear in her novel, *Wuthering Heights*, he is the savage dog, "Tartar," in *Shirley* by her sister, Charlotte, and Emily is the heroine of that book, which followed Charlotte's classic, *Jane Eyre*.

Paul Bransom

They made a strange pair, Keeper and the delicate Emily. The curate, paying a call, regarded them disapprovingly and observed that ladies generally liked lap dogs. Firmly Emily replied: "Perhaps I am an exception."

But an air of apprehension hung over the Brontë house hold. Keeper had a bad habit: he persisted in springing up and reposing on clean beds, and Emily vowed she would break him of it. None doubted she would try. A while ago she had given a pan of water to a slavering dog which wandered to the door. He proved to be rabid and sank his teeth in her hand. The girl ran to the fireplace, snatched out a red-hot poker, cauterized the bite and prevented infection. Yet punishing Keeper was a grave matter. That warning was fresh in every one's mind. "Never strike him or he will fly at your throat."

The day came when Keeper was reported taking his ease on the best bed in the parsonage. In fear and trembling, the family watched Emily enter, pale but with her mouth set, her eyes blazing. She seized the big dog by the scruff of the neck and dragged him, growling ferociously, downstairs. In the corner behind the stairway, she released him and beat him again and again with small, clenched fists. Keeper stood, utterly stupefied, until his mistress led him away and weepingly bathed his bruises. He never bore her a grudge.

When she was only thirty, Emily, never strong, became fatally ill. On the last day of her life in 1848 she insisted on braving the December cold to feed Keeper as usual outdoors. That evening she died. Along with the family, the dog followed her coffin to the grave and sat quietly in the church through the service. Then he lay down outside the door of her bedroom, howling piteously. Until his death three years later, he visited the room daily to snuff and whine for his lost mistress.

"Let us somehow hope, in half Red Indian creed, that he follows Emily now," wrote Mrs. Gaskell, the Brontës' biographer, "and, when he rests, sleeps on some soft, white bed of dreams, unpunished when he awakens to the life of the land of shadows."

PRITCHARD

THE HUNTING DOG OF DUMAS

PRITCHARD was a Scotch Pointer. So said the friend who gave him to Alexandre Dumas, the great French novelist, and probably Pritchard's family tree did include a Pointer, not to mention a Setter, a Scotch Terrier, and several other breeds. At any rate, the gray-white nondescript with pointed ears and a feathery tail was avowed to be a sporting dog. Dumas turned him over to a gamekeeper for training.

Four times Pritchard played hookey. He jumped a four foot fence, chewed leash and collar in two, scratched and gnawed through doors and ran home to the Dumas chateau, where there was more to eat and better company—four other dogs, three monkeys, a cat, a tame vulture, and plenty of poultry. Finally his master let him stay, concluding that he was more talented as a deceiver than as a retriever.

Pritchard stole roasts from the table. He raided the sugar and got his head stuck in the bowl. But soon his hunting heritage asserted itself. He was caught pointing hens, waiting patiently till they laid, then gulping down the eggs. When eggs failed to satisfy Pritchard's appetite, he dined on chicken. Ruefully his master recorded: "I have a dog and I had fowls."

Dumas refused to condemn the guilty one to death. "I think God is equally concerned with man, and with the animals to which He has given life," he wrote. "But perhaps God has a special leaning toward the dog, for of all animals it is the one to which He has given an instinct that comes closest to the intelligence of man." Pritchard had been tempted and he had fallen. To err was equally as canine as human, and to forgive divine.

To stray dogs wandering into the Dumas estate, Pritchard was the soul of hospitality. The novelist watched him welcome them and imagined their conversation.

Stranger: Have you a good master?

Pritchard: Not bad.

Stranger: Are you well feel in your house?

Pritchard: Yes, pâtés twice a day, bones for breakfast and dinner, and in the intervals what you can steal from the kitchen.

Guests could not resist such a rosy prospect. Dumas' valet in despair complained that thirteen dogs had quartered themselves in the chateau, that they would eat an ox, horns and all, and he had best get rid of them all.

"That's an unlucky number," Dumas answered. "Get one more and there will be fourteen." But the expense grew so large that finally all the dogs were ousted but Pritchard.

Finally Pritchard decided really to justify his sporting reputation. He stalked and pointed rabbits so expertly that the game, whether through fright or astonishment at Pritchard's appearance, allowed themselves to be knocked over with a stick. Not even the loss of a hind paw in a trap handicapped the dog; balancing himself on two legs, he lifted a forepaw at the point.

Paul Brown

A dog fight was the death of Pritchard. Dumas mourned him as a remarkable character and made him the hero of a book, *Histoire de Mes Bêtes*. So Pritchard joined the immortal company of *The Three Musketeers* and *The Count of Monte Cristo*.

GREYFRIAR'S BOBBY

SYMBOL OF FAITHFULNESS

No longer Hobby scurried over the Pentland Hills, help-ing Jock Gray herd the flocks. The shepherd, bent by years and illness, had bid heathery pastures farewell and come to a cheap Edinburgh lodging house to end his days. And the Skye Terrier, as always, had followed his master.

Bobby followed still on that day in 1858 when the body of Auld Jock was carried to Greyfriar's Church for burial. The great of Scotland were entombed in crypts within its walls, but there was room for the humble in the churchyard. Chief and almost the only mourner, the small shaggy dog watched while a minister spoke the service, and the earth was heaped over the old shepherd. Then Bobby lay down on the mound.

Sexton James Brown found him there next morning and drove him away. No dogs allowed was the rule. At dusk, the little terrier crept back, only to be turned out again. Day after day the performance was repeated until the sexton's kind heart overruled his duty, and he let Bobby stay. For a while he tied the dog under shelter, but Bobby howled so dismally he was released to return to his master's grave. Finally Brown placed

a mat on the mound and erected a small canopy to give some
protection from the weather. The keeper of an inn nearby
fed the dog, and soon the little creature appeared daily at the
kitchen for his meals. When he learned the inn was closed
Sundays, he saved scraps from Saturday and hid them under
a tombstone to tide him over. Visitors in an increasing stream
came to Greyfriar's to gaze at Bobby, always at his post except
when he left for food. The story of his fidelity drew pilgrims
from as far away as London, then from the United States.
Bobby's fame soared still higher when he was taken to court
for lacking a license. The Lord Provost himself dismissed the
summons and presented him with a collar, marked with his
name. A noted artist painted his portrait, though the Skye
would not remain in the studio for long sittings but insisted on
returning to his master. Engravings sold widely, and Bobby's
story was told in magazines and books.

For fourteen years, through winter's cold and summer heat,
the "wee, leal Hielander" kept his vigil. Finally he succumbed
on his master's grave. The Kirk Sessions gave unprecedented
consent to the dog's burial in consecrated ground beside Auld
Jock. To a rose-bush, marking the spot, later was added a
headstone, the gift of Americans. Near the church stands a
drinking-fountain, a tribute from Baroness Burdett-Coutts;
a life-size statue of Bobby surmounts its granite pillar, and at
its base is a small bowl for thirsty dogs.

To this day, many journey to Edinburgh in memory of
Greyfriar's Bobby. His collar is kept in the church, and there
you may find these touching words in a pamphlet:

"We are taught that dogs have no place in Paradise. But one
cannot read the story of Greyfriar's Bobby without wishing
to round it off with a meeting in the other world between the

shepherd and his dog. After all why may we not hope that, cut low in the very doors of Heaven, there may be a little dog hole through which Bobby and such as he may pass unchallenged? They have brought gifts to God's treasury. They have shown mankind how to be faithful."

SULTAN

DICKENS' BAD DOG

SULTAN was built like a lion and like the roaring one in the Bible walked about, seeking whom he might devour. Presented when a puppy to Charles Dickens, Sultan began by attempting to gulp dawn the famous English novelist's favorite kitten. That was only the first of a long series of misdeeds in his wild and reprehensible career.

Dickens dubbed his new pet a "Spanish Mastiff," but in fact Sultan was a cross between a St. Bernard and a Bloodhound. An earnest and patient effort to make him behave was exerted by his master, who loved dogs. The great story-teller owned many, including one with the truly Dickensian name of Snittle Timberry, and dogs of all degrees trot through the pages of his books. But buff Sultan was a problem pet, and soon his owner was compelled to write: "Sultan has grown amazingly. He is a sight. But he is so accursedly fierce to other dogs that I am obliged to take him out, muzzled. He has taken an invincible repugnance to soldiers; which in a military district like this is inconvenient. Such is his spirit that, with his muzzle tight on, yesterday, he dashed into a company of infantry marching past our house, and pulled down one private. Except under such provocation, he is as gentle and docile with me as a dog can possibly be."

Dickens explained the "provocation" with a smile. Before Sultan was given him by an Irish friend, the dog must have joined the Fenians, a turbulent society formed to fight for the freedom of Erin. Consequently Sultan was bound to attack British uniforms, or anyone in scarlet, with fury.

Kittens and soldiers of the King by no means were Sultan's only victims. He savagely mauled neighbors' dogs. Once a prowler invaded the grounds of Gadshill and barely escaped with his life from the onrush of the St. Bernard-Bloodhound. Dickens' congratulation of his alert watchdog was cut short. He was hard pressed to defend two constables, belatedly arriving, from Sultan's assaults.

Claims for damages, caused by Sultan, mounted higher and higher. Dickens, whose writings and lecturing had made him wealthy, paid up readily. However, thrift learned in his poverty-stricken youth never had left him, and he grudged this constant and considerable outlay. Sultan was well-fed, but he was also eating up far too many book royalties.

A savage act one day in 1867 was the last straw. A little girl skipped toward Dickens' house for a look at the beloved author of *A Christmas Carol*. Sultan knew her-she was the daughter of one of the servants--but he charged down on her, barking fiercely. When the child screamed and ran, the huge dog fastened his fangs on her leg. Though she was rescued from worse injury, her assailant was justly condemned to death. Dickens, deeply distressed, delegated the execution to an armed party, headed by the gardener. Sultan had just commenced to suspect

Paul Brown

that a stroll through the woods with men carrying a shotgun and pushing a wheelbarrow boded him no good, when a shot rang out, and he paid for his crimes.

Sadly the novelist wrote his pet's eulogy: "He was the finest dog I ever saw. Between me and him was a perfect understanding. But to adopt a popular phrase, the understanding between us was so very confidential that it 'went no further.'"

TSCHINGEL

CLIMBER OF THE ALPS

TRUDGING toward the mountain peak he was about to scale, Christian Almer, a noted Swiss Alpine guide, glanced over his shoulder at the six-month-old puppy he had bought for ten francs, as he passed through a village. Red-brown with white markings, the little mongrel resembled a Beagle, with a dash of Spaniel. So far she was following him faithfully. When the ascent became difficult, she could easily be carried.

But the puppy, her short, sturdy legs pumping like pistons, needed no help. She dug her sharp claws into the ice and forged upward. When the climbers cut footholds in steep, slippery slopes, the dog took them like a veteran Alpinist. Some days later, she accompanied a party across the 9000-foot Tschingel Pass and won herself a reputation and a name.

However, Almer had purchased Tschingel as a watch-dog, not as a mountaineer. She took up domestic duties, becoming the mother of thirty-four pups, until in 1868, when she was three, she was given to W. A. B. Coolidge. That young American, a student at Oxford, had taken up mountain-climbing for his health. Tschingel, trotting at his heels, returned to her destiny.

No peak was too lofty, no climb too perilous for Tschingel. Only when she was given some article to guard could she be left at home, and then she was in danger of starving, since few dared approach her and her charge, even to shove food hastily through the door. Every towering mountain was a challenge to Tschingel. Clearly she shared the elation of her human companions when the party reached the summit and seemed as rapt as they at the view. Tireless after a long climb, she bounded over the snow in pursuit of chamois.

Once she nearly met the fate of other daring climbers. On an icy grade, she slipped and could not halt her slide toward death over the brink of a precipice. Fortunately a porter caught her by the collar as she skidded by. The undaunted Tschingel happily continued climbing. If the risk were so great that the party roped themselves together, the rope was passed through the dog's collar behind Miss Marguerite Brevoort, Coolidge's aunt, of whom Tschingel was as fond as of her master. Other wise she ran free, scouting ahead.

Not a few times she prevented loss of lives or serious accidents. She could sense storms brewing; when Tschingel refused to budge, her friends learned to stay under shelter. When she spotted a snow-masked crevasse or loose rock in the path, the alert scout barked or whined a warning, always to be trusted. But if the danger were a poised avalanche, which even a whisper might dislodge, the extraordinary creature froze in a point, as rigid and silent as the best bird-dog's in the hunting field.

Coolidge declared that Tschingel actually wept when she saw him or her other companions caught in a hazardous position. There came an occasion when he discovered she would give her life for his. Master and dog faced each other across an ice-bridge. She would not cross and whined, pleading with

Paul Bransom

him not to attempt it. The Alpinist tested it, decided it was safe. Before he could venture, Tschingel ran out on the ice. It gave way, and the dog plunged down to disappear in the depths of an abyss. As Coolidge, grief-stricken, was reporting her loss at camp, Tschingel plodded in, miraculous survivor of a fall that would have killed any man.

One mighty peak after another was climbed by Tschingel. She was ten years old when incredulous watchers stared upward through telescopes to behold her scaling Mont Blanc, 15,782 feet, with her party. Her dress collar grew heavy with silver pendants, inscribed with the names of thirty peaks and thirty-six passes she had conquered—several of them first ascents. A great climber bestowed this accolade on her: "Miss Tschingel, Honorary Member of the Alpine Club, a mongrel bitch."

Gentle, affectionate, Tschingel lived out her life, enjoying in her leisure a sup of red wine or a dish of weak tea. She died of old age in 1875. Not until thirty-five years later could her master bear to own another dog.

Tschingel's fame remains a by-word among all Alpinists. In Switzerland, her paw-prints, photographs, and plaques are cherished mementos in many a home and inn.

OWNEY

THE POST OFFICE DOG

CLERKS of the Albany, New York, post office, found a little mongrel curled up on a mail sack one morning in 1888. A wistful wag of his tail won him a share of their lunch. They could not bear turning the thin, shivering creature out into the cold. Adopted and named Owney, the dog stayed until the day when the sack he used as a bed was picked up and filled with letters. He followed it into a mail car. Owney was off on his celebrated travels.

Though he was soon sent back to Albany, his post office friends bought him a collar, marked with his name and address, in case he strayed again. It was a wise precaution. Owney, gripped by the travel urge, soon began boarding trains at every opportunity. Mail-car clerks enjoyed his company. Cared for like a registered letter, Owney "mailed" himself to most of the cities and large towns of the United States, with excursions into Canada and Mexico, and his pals of the postal service "postmarked" him by attaching tags to his collar. Trip after trip hung so much weight on the dog's neck that the Postmaster General presented him with a special harness to carry tags

Paul Brown

and conferred on him a frank entitling him to ride free with the U. S. mail. The city of San Francisco added a traveling bag, fitted with a comb and brush, and a dog-blanket.

Owney, returning from a jaunt to Alaska in 1895, was visiting Tacoma, Washington, when he was observed eying mail sacks being loaded aboard the S.S. Victoria with a calculating look which seemed to say, "Mails go abroad. Why shouldn't I?" Friends hastily provided him with a letter of introduction to postal people everywhere, and he trotted up the gangplank. Making the voyage as the captain's guest, Owney landed in Japan, where he was received and decorated by the Mikado. The Emperor of China similarly honored him, as did personages all along his homeward route via the Suez Canal and at European ports. More than 200 medals and scrolls crammed Owney's baggage when his ship docked in New York. There the globe-trotter without delay caught an express for the west and reached Tacoma, his starting point, to establish a canine record of circling the world in 132 days. Like some human celebrities, Owney became over-impressed with his own importance and he grew cranky and irritable in his old age. The wanderlust was still on him, and while he was no longer the pleasant traveling companion he had been, he was allowed to accompany the mails until in 1897 he bit a postal clerk and had to be destroyed. His mounted hide in the Smithsonian Institution, Washington, commemorates the days when he was the mascot of the U.S. Post Office and as welcome everywhere as a letter with good news.

HANDSOME DAN

YALE BULLDOG

A GRIMY Bulldog, standing in the doorway of a black-smith's shop, caught the eyes of a group of college students strolling by. Andrew B. Graves, of the Yale Class of 1892, Sheffield Scientific School, stopped and made friends with him. That appealingly ugly, compressed mug and the stubby, wagging tail were irresistible. Graves bought the dog and gave him a bath.

It was a fine, pure-white animal that emerged from the tub and shook his hide vigorously--all white except for brown head markings. The underslung jowl, ferocious scowl, and super-bowlegs of his kind, bred to fight bulls, prevented any rating as a thing for beauty. He looked like "a cross between an alligator and a horned toad." His master by way of compensation named him Handsome Dan.

Since Graves was a crew substitute and a football rooter, Handsome Dan began attending Yale athletic events, and soon none was complete without him. At Harvard games, his special glory, the white Bulldog would be led across the gridiron, swaggering along at his bow-legged, rolling gait. Ordered to speak to the enemy, he would defy the Crimson stands with fierce

Paul Brown

grimaces and angry harks. From the sidelines he watched the game intently, growling savagely at Harvard ball-carriers and straining to break loose for a flying tackle at the seat of their pants. It was boasted that the Harvard team for years owed its continued existence to the fact that Handsome Dan's leash held.

Out of the sports season, Handsome Dan condescended to be exhibited at dog shows where, competing against imported English entries, he won scores of awards. But his proudest title was that of Yale mascot and symbol, celebrated in story, art, and Cole Porter's bulldog song, which revives Handsome Dan's memory at football games today.

When Graves left law school for a foreign tour, which would become a lifelong Paris residence as a banker, he took his pet along. Dan died in England, and his hide was stuffed and presented to the Yale trophy room. He lived on, as dogs do, in his master's heart. During the Second World War, Graves, who had stayed in Paris through the German occupation, was visited by a Yale man, an officer in the American army of liberation. They talked of Handsome Dan, and the old alumnus gave the younger one portraits, autographed by him, of the famous Yale Bulldog.

Meanwhile a dynasty had been founded. In 1932 another white Bulldog, Handsome Dan II, was acquired as the Yale mascot. It was his fate to be dognapped by reprehensible Harvard men, retaliating for a raid by the Blue, and photographed licking the hamburg-smeared feet of the statue of John Harvard.

The Graves estate gave mementos of Handsome Dan to the Yale Club of New York City: a portrait of the mascot, scowling ferociously as he used to do when he was urging a Yale crew to pull ahead or a fullback to plunge through the line for a touchdown; nine silver medals awarded him by the Bull Dog

Club of America at shows in New York, Boston, and Washington from 1891 to 1895—Best Novice, Best American Bred Bull Dog, Best American Bred Dog. Prized most highly was the Yale-blue blanket Dan always wore at athletic events. Still clinging to its underside were white hairs he had shed, hairs his fond master never could bear to brush off.

Other Yale Bulldogs followed at intervals in the line of succession, until in 1949 Handsome Dan VI was ruling. But none, in the opinion of old graduates who knew the original, has matched Handsome Dan I.

LION

A DOGSTAR

"My dear, they say the dog in this play is simply wonderful!"

Such praise always echoed through the crowded houses at *Hans, the Boatman—An Idyll of the Adirondacks,* as the orchestra tuned up for the overture. Charles Arnold was the star of that musical drama, a tremendous hit of 1897 and for some years afterwards. But the big St. Bernard, Lion, in the part of "Towser," stole the show whenever he came on stage. Lion, a conscientious actor, was always waiting in the wings for his cues and never needed any prompting. So much of the action hinged on him that the play would have collapsed had he failed.

Hans, the Boatman, by Clay M. Greene, was a tear-jerker, which in a later, more sophisticated day would be described as "corn straight off the cob." Its hero goes blind and is estranged from his wife. The trusty "Towser" reunites them. In time for a happy ending, "Hans" recovers his sight, and the dog senses that his master, who had come to depend on him, now no longer needs him so greatly. Lion played the scene, in which that

Paul Brown

distressing knowledge dawns upon him, to the hilt. His sad expression, characteristic of St. Bernards, took on intensity, and he stood before the footlights a picture of utter despondency, while the audience wept buckets. Then "Hans" laid a hand on the majestic, shaggy head and delivered a line in German-American dialect that brought down the house:

"De richest man in de vorld could not buy vun vag of his dear old tail!"

In several road companies, other St. Bernards were assigned the part of "Towser," but it was Lion that was chosen to make two world tours in the drama's long run. Besides England and the United States, they took him to India, South Africa, Japan, and Australia. Before he retired he made a travel record, rivaled only by Owney, the post office dog.

PETER SPOTS

FIRE DOG ON PROBATION

"MAD dog! Mad dog!"

Just ahead of a gang of shouting boys, flourishing sticks and stones, a streak of white hide flecked with black flashed through the fire-house door. The young toughs would have rushed in and finished off their victim, if a fireman had not reached for a whip and driven them away.

Trembling with terror under the hose tower cringed a Dalmatian. A fireman, disregarding a comrade's warning, went over to him with a gruff, "Not mad--just scared." They treated his injured hind leg and fed him. Washed, the black spots stood on his smooth body. His head and ears were jet except for the white of his muzzle running up to a peak between his eyes. The grizzled captain, strolling in, bent over the handsome animal.

"Like to be a fireman's dog? What's your name?"

A lolling tongue twitched, as if the dog was striving to answer.

"That ain't loud enough," the captain chided. "What's your name?" And now he drew a short, eager bark.

"Sounds like Pete," one of the rescuing firemen interpreted.

Then and there the new arrival was formally enrolled as a fireman of the third grade under the name of Peter Spots. This dog of the breed originating in Dalmatia, called after that Austrian province and known also as the English Coach Dog, the Carriage Dog, and the Plum Pudding Dog, gained that day his breed's fifth and proudest title--The Fire House Dog.

It took Peter a little time to break in. The bells of the first alarm he heard drove him to refuge in the furnace of the spare engine, and the captain threatened to have him up before the commissioners and fined five days' pay. But that run was the only one he missed. Thereafter he took his place under the truck of the engine, ears and tail up. As door swung open, Peter dashed out, clearing people from the sidewalk. Speeding at least half a block ahead of the galloping team, his shrill barking opened a right of way through streets' intersections better than the clanging gong and whistle of the apparatus thundering behind. At blazes Peter climbed ladders with his fellow firemen, though he could not descend, and when he got his "dose" of smoke and was overcome, he had to be carried down. Once a heavy hose stream swept him off a high sill, but he fell into snow and was only a little lamed. Again he was drenched in zero weather but took it as part of the day's work; firemen insisted that he would have wagged his tail except it was frozen stiff.

Unfortunately Peter became too zealous. Dalmatians and horses traditionally are firm friends, and it was only in a helpful spirit that Peter took to biting at the chests of green fire horses to hurry them into place at the pole. Worse still, he caused further delay by nipping at them to speed them up in the run. His company was several times beaten to a blaze by its rival, which got "first water." After a bawling out by the

chief, the captain put Peter on probation and told the firemen they'd best get rid of him. Sorrowfully Peter was confined to the shop of a neighborhood baker.

Peter liked bread but how dull it was after the firehouse. Came the day when the street outside resounded to clanging bells and galloping hoofs. That was more than Peter Spots could bear. He jumped into the display window, wreaking havoc on cakes and pies. As the engine rolled past, he backed away and launched himself at the glass-paned door. A shattering crash, and the fire dog was in front of his company, sharp and penetrating bark clearing the way as of yore.

Happily reinstated, Peter Spots took his tour of house watch, sitting alertly in a chair by the telegraph and quick to sound off when his company's signal rang. No longer did he bite horses and he never failed to make the runs. But if he ever discovered that it was a bakery going up in smoke, the company had to do without him. Peter abruptly and hastily went home.

PETER CHAPIN

A BOOK RETRIEVER

WEN the black Cocker Spaniel came to Howard Millar Chapin's home, he had to start—literally and figuratively—from scratch. Cats, especially the favorite Murthy, resented canine intrusion. Peter, outnumbered, kept his distance and bided his time. Just as the dog began making headway, the master's attention was distracted by a girl. They got married and went away together, leaving Peter behind in lonely despair.

After their return from the honeymoon, Peter's demonstrations of joy far surpassed the cats' contained welcome. Although Chapin, a historian, had compiled a book about cats, called *Murthy's Cattage,* now he turned to writing about dogs of early New England--about Martin Pring's Foole and Gallant and the two that landed on Plymouth Rock, one of them a Spaniel. Perhaps Peter could thus be listed as a *Mayflower* descendant; at least the claim could be made as well for him as for some of the many humans who boasted it.

The Chapins, proving childless, lavished their affection on Peter. Never again was he left alone at home but accompanied them on their many trips abroad in spite of the difficulty of foreign travel with a dog. He became a well-known dog-about-town in Paris, where he took bows from a hotel balcony or

Paul Brown

strolled along the boulevards, his long ears tied up over his head to keep them out of dust or mud. Seated at train windows, he enjoyed passing sights with keen interest. He frolicked through Italy like the Brownings' Flush. When his owners and he were marooned in that country by World War I, and no funds could be obtained from home, they were given hospitality by an Italian nobleman. Although their host had originally been moved by enthusiasm for *Murthy's Cattage*, he succumbed to Peter's charm and helped arrange the Chapins' repatriation.

Many acquaintances of the globe-trotting Peter began sending his master and mistress books and pamphlets on dogs. Once started, the collection was added to by the family and grew steadily. Peter, become a book dog instead of a bird dog, was given credit for retrieving many a rare volume.

Peter died at the ripe old age for dogs of fourteen years and was buried under a granite slab. Yet the stone seemed as inadequate to perpetuate his memory as were other dogs to fill the place of his fond companionship. Then was born the idea of increasing the book collection and making it Peter's memorial. This labor of love filled the rest of the Chapins' lives. They assembled scarce and valuable items—the great dog stories and poems—histories of noted packs--stud books and treatises on breeds-works on hunting and dog racing--many beautifully illustrated volumes. The Peter Chapin Collection of Books on Dogs was presented to the College of William and Mary, Williamsburg, Virginia, where it draws questions from all over the world, ranging from breeding and training to inquiries on the use of dogs for churning.

None of the books is about Peter. But with his portrait as the bookplate of a great collection he appears in twenty-three hundred of them.

RIN TIN TIN

MASCOT AND MOVIE STAR

Oᴏᴛ of the flaming wreckage of an American plane, shot down near Metz in the First World War, soldiers dragged a brown Alsatian, the aviator's mascot. Soon afterwards she produced a litter of five, sire-probably a German Shepherd--unknown. One of the pups, which had made this dramatic entrance into the world, was adopted by another flier, Lieut. Lee L. Duncan.

Duncan named his pet Rin Tin Tin after one of the pair of little worsted dolls, carried by many French people as good luck charms against shells and bombs, and raised him on condensed milk. Rin flew with his master and stayed close by his side when pneumonia put the officer in a hospital. Duncan, mustered out and sent home, took his dog, which would prove to be one of the most valuable war souvenirs ever annexed.

On the small ranch bought by Duncan near Santa Monica, California, Rin learned to herd sheep and to jump hedges and other obstacles. A newsreel camera man, happening by, made a film of the dog's beautiful hurdling. When the impromptu screen test was seen by the Warner Brothers, motion-picture

Paul Brown

producers, Rin was promptly signed to a contract and given the lead in his first picture. Under Duncan's skilled coaching, a dog star, the brightest of them all, rose in the Hollywood skies.

Rin's pictures were smash hits. At first there was difficulty in persuading him to rescue heroines from dastardly villains, because the screen bad men had made friends with him in the studio, and the dog refused to attack them before the camera. Kept aloof thereafter, Rin assaulted villainous strangers with such savage realism that their suits had to be padded. In one thriller, he fought a vulture in a duel to the death on the brink of a precipice. A lion movie actor fled before him without staying to stage even a token fight. Since scripts called for him always to win, Rin developed an exaggerated idea of his prowess until off the lot one day he charged a bus and was nearly killed.

Some of Rin's screen plays were written by Darryl F. Zanuck, later a noted producer. Myrna Loy and Charles Farrell, future stars, played secondary leads in his casts. He made more than $300,000 for his owner, and his pictures are said to have grossed fifteen million dollars. His fan mail ran to 2000 letters a week; all were answered and signed by the print of his paw.

Handsome though he was, Rin, like other actors, required a make-up man; one of his ears drooped and had to be taped erect. When a mate was selected for him, he rejected her for a German Shepherd named Nanette, met on a train trip. His acting always was better when she was present on the lot and better still when Nanette played in a picture with him.

Rin's career struck its first snag when silent films gave way to sound. No longer could Duncan call out the commands the dog obeyed so readily. The trainer solved the problem by devising a signal system. When his master, standing behind the camera, held up a black velvet cat, Rin registered rage. A toy lion called for incessant barking, and a woolly rabbit for tail wagging.

For ten years, Rin was one of the biggest attractions in the movies, rivaling Rudolf Valentino in his prime. When he died at the age of fourteen, he was buried on an estate, bought from his earnings by his master, and a single white rose bush planted over his grave.

His name, his military heritage, and his cinema fame were carried on by his family. His son, Rin Tin Tin II, succeeded him as a star but had completed only two pictures when he lost his life in an accident. The second Rin's mate became a war dog and was killed in action in the South Pacific jungles. One of their pups, Rin III, served as a drill sergeant in a K-9 Corps training camp and afterwards took up his grand father's film career. Meanwhile, making certain that the dynasty remained unbroken, a puppy of the next generation, Rin Tin Tin IV, waited in the wings.

LAD

DOG STORY HERO

L$_{AD}$ was an eighty-pound collie, thoroughbred in spirit as well as blood. He had the benign dignity that was a heritage from endless generations of high strain ancestors. He had, too, the gay courage of a d'Artagnan, and an uncanny wisdom. Also--who could doubt it, after a look into his mournful brown eyes--he had a Soul."

Thus Albert Payson Terhune began a story about his handsome dog with a coat of "orange-flecked mahogany." Lad not only inspired the tale but sold it, acting as his master's literary agent.

A noted magazine editor, Ray Long, had come to see Terhune at his home, Sunnybank, in New Jersey. Lad, usually reserved and aloof, made great friends with this stranger, and Long, succumbing to the big Collie's charm, urged his host, "Write me a story about Lad."

Terhune demurred, insisting that the public wanted he-and-she stuff. But one humors important editors, and he wrote the story. Readers demanded more. Soon there were enough of these tales, largely based on actual adventures of Lad's, for a

Paul Brown

book. Although a book about dogs was a risky venture in 1919, a publisher chanced it and gasped, as the sales soared. *Lad: a Dog* passed the 50,000 mark in ten years and continues to sell. More books, stories, and articles about the gallant Lad and other dogs followed, earning many thousands of dollars for the author. The time came when Terhune had to include a Collie in every piece he wrote, whether one properly belonged in it or not.

Lad, which at first had had only one canine companion, became the patriarch of a pack of Collies, each one a living dog story. They roamed through the hills with their tall, husky master on hikes and hunting and fishing trips. Challenged that the dogs he bred were good for literary purposes only, Terhune entered them in the big kennel-club shows, and they carried off scores of blue ribbons.

Clubs of Lad's admirers were formed all over the country. His fans, swarms of children as well as adults, flocked to Sunnybank in such numbers that strict visiting hours had to be established. Lad received homage in dignified tolerance, far preferring to be alone with his worshiped master and mistress. When Mrs. Terhune recovered from a serious illness, during which Lad kept a long, devoted vigil, lying outside her door, the gentlemanly, well-behaved Collie reacted from the strain with what Bert Terhune described as a terrific spree. He broke into the dairy and spilled milk pans. He chased every cow, horse, and cat on the place and thrashed two younger dogs. He went on a rampage among the clothes lines and stole a roast of lamb from the kitchen. Finally he dug up an ancient, treasured bone and walked into his mistress's bedroom, tail tremulous with affection and relief, to lay his gift on her lap.

After a long, full life of sixteen years, loving and beloved,

Lad died quietly in his sleep. "Lad's fame," modestly wrote his master, "was due to his own greatness and not to any clumsy yarns I wrote about him." His monument bears the inscription: "Lad: Thoroughbred in Body and Soul." Pilgrims from many States, Canada, and England came, as they had in his lifetime, and visited his grave.

JIGGS

MARINE MASCOT

THE Army had its mule mascot, with a kick like the impact of a howitzer shell. A sudden butt from the horned head of the Navy goat was not to be taken lightly by any target. The Marine Corps, needing a fighting animal to serve as its symbol, found him when Jiggs enlisted two years after the end of the First World War.

A big white Bulldog, with a jaw that could gape like a steam shovel and close like a vise, Jiggs looked the part of a *Teufelhund*—devil dog—the nickname given Marines by Germans, who had met them in combat in France. But Jiggs, though ready to fight if he had to, was normally gentle in disposition like other good warriors. He did full duty and never was brought up before a court martial for any breach of regulations. His rise through the ranks was rapid for peace time. In 1924 he was promoted to sergeant major by order of the Secretary of the Navy.

On parade, besides his collar and harness, Jiggs wore a dress uniform consisting of a blanket bearing U.S.M.C. in large letters, the globe and anchor insignia, his chevrons, and a "hash

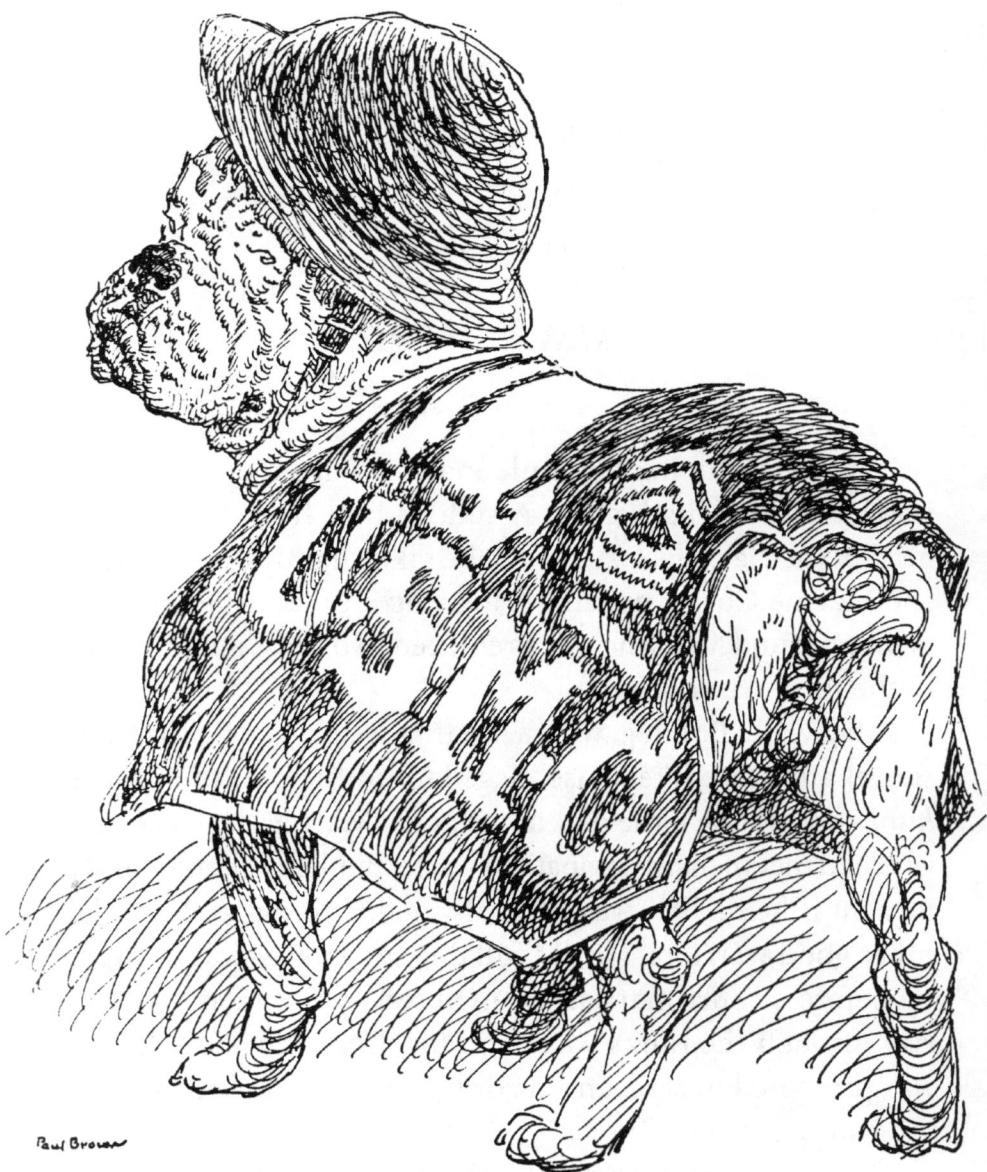

Paul Brown

mark" or service stripe. His record card showed thousands of miles of travel by land, water, and air; he always accompanied Marine football and baseball teams. At Army Navy games he swaggered along the sidelines, a football or steel helmet or a campaign hat cocked on his massive head. Once he was presented at the White House. When Jiggs died in 1927, a bomber with a guard of honor took his body to Quantico, Virginia, Marine base, for burial.

Jiggs founded a dynasty, as did Handsome Dan, the Yale Bulldog. Gene Tunney, former Marine and heavyweight boxing champion, gave the Corps Jiggs II. He, unlike his predecessor, stood trial on a charge and was found guilty of loitering and chasing rabbits in the danger zone of the rifle range. Later mascots were the gifts of the British Royal Marines and a Marine's widow. The line of Leatherneck Bulldogs will carry on, ready like their masters to fight their country's battles "from the halls of Montezuma to the shores of Tripoli."

BOBBIE

A HOMING HEART

Bobbie was a Collie, plus a dash of English Sheep Dog. When he was six weeks old, he was acquired by G. Frank Brazier, a restaurant man of Silverton, Oregon. In puppyhood, Bobbie learned that deep, abiding love of his family and his home that throbs in the heart of a dog, aware that he in turn is cherished. That was the first of the compelling urges which made possible the extraordinary feat Bobbie would perform.

Others were his courage and persistence. True to his breed strains, Bobbie was a working dog. He liked to help herd horses. One day a crotchety nag, annoyed at being driven toward the stable, kicked him twenty feet. Bobbie shook his bleeding head, which would bear a scar for life, got up and finished ushering the stubborn horse into its stall. Next he was struck by a tractor and so badly injured his owner considered putting him out of his misery. But Bobbie, refusing to give up and die, recovered.

In 1923, his family rejoiced him by taking him on a long automobile trip. Driving east from Oregon, they stopped at a garage in an Indiana town. A local dog sighted Bobbie in the car and barked insulting remarks. Bobbie scrambled out and in a far-ranging scrap convinced the canine Hoosier that politeness to strangers is a virtue. The Braziers, ready to motor on, searched vainly for their pet. Sadly, leaving reward offers for

Paul Brown

his return, they drove on. They toured south to Mexico, thence to California and up the coast back to their home in Oregon. Losing a dog is a tragedy no easier to bear from the fact it happens to many. Months passed, and the Braziers gave up hope.

But Bobbie was determined not to stay lost. After his fight he returned to the garage to find his family gone. Perhaps he first followed the trail of the car's tires by scent. Anyway, he trotted south.

Mile after weary mile, he plodded on his trek. His quest led him across the prairies, through towns and farms, into swamps, skirting lakes, over the hot sands of desert. Once in the south he strayed from the course he had pursued so surely. An instinct, marvelous as that of the homing pigeon, rescued him and he struck northwest. Often hungry and thirsty, exhausted and footsore, he threaded his way through the streets of large cities—Des Moines--Denver.

People remembered the passing of the gaunt, resolute dog. Now and again, Bobbie stopped at farms where kind women fed him, or approached campfires with wagging tail and won a welcome from woodsmen. Never staying long, he forged on

On February 15, 1924, exactly six months after the day he was lost, a thin, worn Bobbie limped up to his Oregon home. He had traveled 3000 miles!

His overjoyed family reported his return. Spread over front pages, it became a national sensation. People all along his route wrote to confirm the extent of his great journey. Before Bobbie recuperated-it was a week before he could struggle to his feet--he was famous. He was presented with a gold collar and medals galore. A wire-mesh barrier had to be put up to protect him, such were the throngs of his admiring visitors. Some had traveled considerable distance. But then so had Bobbie.

TOGO

A SIBERIAN AND SERUM

THE gray-furred puppy, the only one in his mother's last litter, was so small he hardly seemed worth raising as a sled dog. True, he was of the Siberian breed imported to Alaska a few years ago and already making a name for fleetness and endurance. But this pup was undersized and being spoiled as an only son. Best give him away as a pet. No such life, soft and shut-in, suited the gray Siberian.

He ran away and came back home, back to the kennels of Norwegian-born Leonhard Seppala, one of the great dog drivers of the North. The pup practically forced Seppala to use him by hanging around teams until his master harnessed him in. That first day in draft the eight-month-old covered seventy-five miles and proved himself a first-rate sled dog. More, he soon showed that he was a natural-born leader. Admiringly Seppala named him Togo after the Japanese admiral, also small of stature but mighty in leadership, who was the hero of the war with Russia.

Togo learned to keep his eight-foot lead line taut and hold his team on a straight course through blinding blizzards. Another valuable lesson came to him early when he tackled a team of tough Malamutes and limped home with his gray coat crimsoned with bloody gashes. Thereafter on the trail he always swung his team wide of other hitches and avoided those savage fights which cripple many dogs.

Silver cups and other prizes, racing trophies won by Togo and his teammates, began to line Seppala's shelves. To their credit also stood perilous journeys, all in an Arctic day's work, like the eighty-four-mile drive of two nights and a day across the floes of Norton Bay to rush a prospector with a half-severed leg to the hospital.

Togo's greatest moment came in the Nome, Alaska, diphtheria epidemic of January and February, 1925. Precious serum had given out, and children and adults were dying, as the dread disease clutched at their throats. Except for telephone and telegraph through which its dire need was reported, Nome was isolated by a terrific storm. Only dog teams could reach or leave the stricken city.

A supply of serum was rushed to Nenana, as far as possible by rail. The rest of the journey—an appalling gap of 675 miles—was up to dogs and drivers. Over the wires clicked directions for a team from Nome to mush to meet one bringing the serum from the South.

Anxious Nome chose and pinned its hopes on Driver Seppala. Citizens cheered him as he mushed southward, twelve spare dogs following his team, and the white curtain of the raging snowstorm dropped behind him. Togo trotted proudly in the lead, flaunting his curved, bushy tail. He forged ahead through numbing Arctic cold—30 degrees below zero. Thirty miles lay behind the team the first day; after that they came close to averaging fifty.

Paul Brown

Yonder loomed a dog-team from the south. Seppala took over the serum from its driver, wheeled his team and raced northward, retracing his tracks. With stops only to warm the serum over a fire to prevent freezing, he drove Togo and his mates hard in a ninety-six-mile dash. They then met and handed on their cargo to a team in a string of relays, established to speed the medicine as the emergency grew more acute. So it happened that another driver and team, with a dog named Balto as leader, brought the serum into Nome on the last relay leg.

Togo had led Seppala's dogs in a remarkable dash of 340 miles, four times the distance covered by any other team. But Balto, because he chanced to head the triumphant entry, won acclaim that brought him stage and movie engagements and a statue in Central Park, New York City; honors rightly Togo's.

Worn by the serum drive, getting on in years, Togo was ready to retire, whether or not the world granted him any laurels to rest on. He was even willing to become a pet now. Cherished by a Maine friend of his master's, the small but mighty Siberian died in 1929.

BUDDY

SEEING EYE PIONEER

"THE hearing ear, and the seeing eye, the Lord hath made even both of them."

They were God's gifts to His living creatures, the hearing ear and the seeing eye. But when a woman with a shining face, Dorothy Eustis, quoted that sentence from the Book of Proverbs in the Bible, she was writing about dogs, dogs that could be trained to use their keen hearing and sight to guide human beings, who had lost the second priceless gift--people who were blind.

Seeing Eye Dogs, leading sightless persons through the streets today, are following in the path of the German Shepherd, Buddy, the pioneer.

A fascinating chain of circumstances produced Buddy. Mrs. Eustis, struck by the intelligence of a dog of her own, left the States with her husband to found a training center, "Fortunate Fields," for police and army communications dogs in Switzerland. In 1927, she paid a visit to a school of guide dogs for the blind in Germany. What higher mission could be given the animal, which has been mankind's most devoted friend, since the first wild clog was tamed? The Eustises began concentrating on guide dogs, seconded by the expert trainer, Elliott Humphrey, and Mrs. Eustis wrote a glowing article about the work for an American magazine.

The article was read to Morris Frank, a blind insurance man of Nashville, Tennessee. His eager inquiry brought an invitation from Mrs. Eustis to come to Switzerland for a dog. Through the blackness which was his lot, he made the long journey, often desperately bitter, scarcely daring to hope. On the train approaching his destination, a clergyman in the seat beside him told him of a mountain looming above them: Mount Pelerin, a shrine for pilgrims. Said the minister quietly: "Pilgrims go on faith and so must you."

At "Fortunate Fields," they gave Frank a young German Shepherd female; already it had been recognized that the responsive temperament of bitches made them better guides than male dogs. She was called Kiss. No name for a dog, Frank declared, and changed it to Buddy. Feeding, grooming and petting her, he won her affection. Meanwhile he, too, underwent training, learning both to use and trust his guide and self-reliance. Soon Buddy was leading him surely through Vevey's traffic, while he grasped the handle on her harness. One day as they were walking along a sunken road, a runaway team thundered down on them, with a watching trainer too far behind to help. He was not needed. Instantly Buddy dragged her master up the slope of a steep embankment to safety. Back in the center, Frank lifted his head, and there seemed to be a light in his sightless eyes as he cried, "I'm free!"

Buddy, always at his side, guided him on the trip home, so far different from that groping journey over alone. On landing in New York, a reporter dared the young blind man to cross

Paul Brown

West Street with his dog, and Frank accepted the challenge. Unerring, Buddy led him through the hurly-burly of trucks and drays on that waterfront thoroughfare, then without traffic lights.

They became missionaries, those two, in the great cause they represented: guide dogs for the blind. Their tours helped Mrs. Eustis establish The Seeing Eye at Morristown, New Jersey, where now several hundred trained dogs a year are given the blind. With Buddy, Frank found new zest in life and his business. Once she rescued him from a hotel fire, once from falling through the open door of an elevator shaft. For him she performed constant, clever services: finding lost collar buttons--picking up a dropped match-box-leading him after the porter carrying his bags. She recognized uniforms and would take Frank up to a policeman when he needed directions. An intricate bit of guiding always exhilarated her, and she was plainly proud of herself. Yet she was not all paragon but a perfectly natural dog. She stole cookies, got mixed up with a skunk and could not be broken of climbing on to clean bedspreads and jumping up to place muddy forepaws on a visitor.

Buddy's time came. For no one is the death of a dog a greater tragedy than the owner of a Seeing Eye guide--darkness descends again. But for Frank, as for others of the blind, a successor was waiting. With Buddy II, he regained the freedom and the faith he had found that day in Switzerland.

CHINOOK

SLED DOG IN THE ANTARCTIC

AT a steady pace, Chinook led the six-dog team through a snow-shrouded pass in New Hampshire's White Mountains. Mushing behind the sled, Arthur Walden, expert dog driver, veteran of the Klondike gold rush, proudly gazed ahead at his big leader. Chinook was a cross breed, Walden's own development. His pulling power he owed to his Husky blood, his gentle strength to a St. Bernard forebear. In him also showed the intelligence of the German Shepherd and the traits of other breeds. But his ancestry was his master's secret, for with Chinook as sire, Walden had founded a new and valuable type of sled dog.

Bitter cold and snowy heights were nothing to this team. Driving Chinook and his progeny, Walden in mid-winter had scaled 6000-foot Mount Washington in eight hours.

But the pass the team was threading today was treacherous. Now a sudden avalanche roared down a steep slope. It missed the team and sled but buried the driver to his neck, with one upstretched arm partly free. Walden, packed under so solidly he could not stir, must soon freeze to death.

The team, frightened by the avalanche, had scurried away,

Paul Brown

but Chinook looked over his shoulder and saw the plight of his helpless master. Resolutely, he turned his teammates, led them back and swung the sled close so that Walden could grab a runner with his free hand. The big leader lunged forward. He and all the hitch plunged against their chest straps, tugging until they dragged Walden out of the snow's vise.

Chinook was destined to face still fiercer cold and hardships. When Admiral Byrd sailed for the Antarctic in 19:29, he took Walden as dog trainer, and with the New Hampshire man went Chinook and forty more of the best sled dogs in his kennels.

Through the icy wastes which border the South Pole, Chinook led his team over jagged hummocks, across glassy floes and around perilous crevasses in the toughest mushing of his career. It told on him--he was nearly twelve, old age for a dog, especially a sled dog which has known hard toil since youth. The day came when a younger dog had to be put in Chinook's place. The old fellow knew he was through.

That night, Walden, bundled in his sleeping-bag, twice felt a forepaw softly touch his face. Next morning he realized that a devoted friend had been saying good-by. Chinook had vanished. After the manner of sled dogs, he had wandered off to die alone.

The sturdy breed he sired carries on his name, and through New Hampshire runs a highway, titled in his memory—the Chinook Trail.

CHIPS

HE STORMED A MACHINE GUN

Offspring of a Husky and a Collie-German Shepherd, Chips was tough. He feared neither man nor beast except his sire; the Husky, a stern father, kept the pup in his place. Always Chips was the loyal guardian of his owners, the Wren family of Pleasantville, New York. He followed eight-year-old Gail to school and lay down by her desk, and teachers, who might have shooed out Mary's little lamb, let Gail's sleeping dog lie. Also he was Mrs. Wren's self-appointed escort to the dentist's. Never was drilling and filling more gently done, but if the patient did feel a twinge, she dared not moan, lest the treatment suddenly include Chips' teeth, with the dentist on the receiving end.

Chips was the bane of postmen and bicyclists and he bit the garbageman. He liked to nap at street intersections where cops considerately and prudently detoured traffic around him. A moral force in the community, he snapped at the heels of tipsy townsmen weaving past his house and left them soberer and wiser men.

After the outbreak of the Second World War, the Wrens

decided that Chips' talents were definitely martial and enlisted him in the K-9 Corps. He trained at Front Royal and led the first detachment of four American war dogs overseas. In an amphibious tank, they landed in French Morocco under fire. As they hit the beach, and Chips' handler dug holes for the dog and himself, Vichy planes bombed them. The minute steel fragments stopped whizzing past, the handler jumped up to deepen his foxhole. Chips watched intently--then sand flew under his paws as he scooped his own deeper.

He marched into action with his battalion and did outpost duty through inky African nights, guarding against raiders and plundering Arabs. When President Roosevelt attended the Casablanca conference, Chips walked post as one of his sentries. Off duty, he had a love affair with the K-9 "WAC," Mena. Four of their litter of nine were furloughed home with the mother to star in a dog show; competition for the other five pups as mascots was terrific.

Soon Chips was off to war again. He and Private Rowell, his handler, were members of one of our task forces that landed in Sicily. Barking and whining, the big war dog sighted crimson flames spurting from a camouflaged pillbox. He jerked his leash free. A streak of brown hide, and Chips sprang inside the pillbox. Wild shrieks and murderous growls cut through the tumult of battle. Out staggered an enemy machine gun-ner, a snarling, slashing fury at his throat. The three others of the crew rushed out and surrendered. Chips, burned and wounded in the scalp, was cited for the Silver Star and the Purple Heart and would have been awarded them, had not the War Department ruled against decorations for animals. General Eisenhower himself congratulated him but got nipped when he ventured a pat.

Paul Brown

Chips served on through campaigns in Italy, France, and Germany. By the time he was shipped back to the states, worn and sick, he rated eight battle stars. Proudly, the Wrens welcomed the K-9 veteran home from the wars. His bushy Husky tail, once flaunted like knight's plume, drooped now, and he only growled at the rattle of garbage cans. Loved and honored, Chips was cared for by his family until in 1947, weakened by battle fatigue and ailments, the old warrior's fighting heart gave way.

ANDY

WARDOG, U. S. MARINES

In camp, Andy quickly absorbed the stiff training the Marines gave him. For Andy was a Doberman Pinscher, and his breeding fitted him for the task ahead of him as a scout dog in the Second World War. Keen nose, strength and size (he stood about 28 inches at the shoulder and weighed about 70 pounds). Alertness, distrust of strangers. A jet-black coat, lightening to tan on his legs, which would blend into the dark shadows of the jungle. These were his military qualifications, bequeathed him by the strains Louis Doberman combined to originate his breed: the German Pinscher, the Rottweiller, and the Black and Tan Terrier.

Andy and his handlers, members of the First Marine War Dog Platoon--twenty-four dogs and fifty-five men-hit the beach under heavy fire at Bougainville in the Solomon Islands late in 1943. As they bored into the jungle, Andy was assigned to head a patrol. So well trained he worked off leash, Shakespeare's line, "Let slip the dogs of war," might have been written of him. Out he stepped with the proud stride that had won him the nickname of "Gentleman Jim."

Japanese ambushes waited along that tunnel-like trail, dark and somber even with the sun at high noon. Grim experience had taught the Americans that seldom could a passage be forced without paying for it with lives and wounds. Camouflaged Jap snipers and machine-guns, undetected till they opened fire, would take toll. The Marines skeptically watched Andy up ahead at the point of the patrol. What could a dog do except spring the ambush and get himself and the men with him killed?

Suddenly the scout dog froze in his tracks. His pointed ears pricked sharply, his hackles rose. Trained not to bark, a soft warning growl rumbled in his throat. His head veered toward the right of the trail. Handler Robert Lansley whispered back: "Well, this is it. There's a Japanese sniper back in there, probably about seventy-five yards."

A couple of automatic riflemen crept forward. Shots rattled, and down from a mangrove tree tumbled a dead soldier. Neither the sniper's cover of leaves nor his skin painted green had been able to fool Andy. Like all dogs, he was color-blind, and his sight, quick to catch movement, was excelled by his nose and ears. Twice more that day he alerted to the presence of snipers. The company he led advanced farther than any other.

The Marines drove deeper into the island, with Andy and other war dogs making a splendid record. Kuno, a Doberman, was mortally wounded in action. A German Shepherd, Caesar, also was hit while giving warning and helping to rout a dawn attack by the Japs. On the fourteenth day of the fight, Andy, leading another jungle patrol, halted and moved forward sideleggedly—his way of saying there was enemy in force up ahead. Lansley crawled toward two big banyan trees. Hidden among their roots were Japanese machine-guns, set to deliver

Ian Brown

a murderous cross-fire on the trail. Marine machine-gunners slipped up and blasted them out. Lansley and his comrades raced in, hurling hand grenades into dugouts beneath the trees. All along the sector, American lines, which would have been held up, advanced.

Andy and five other dogs of the platoon were cited in orders, and the Commandant of the Marine Corps wrote letters of congratulation to the owners who had given them to serve their country. Despatches repeatedly declared: "No patrols led by dogs were fired on first or suffered casualties." Especially in the Pacific but on other fronts as well, hundreds of American lives were saved by scout, messenger and sentry dogs.

Andy never came home, but it wasn't a Japanese sniper that got him. He was struck and mortally injured by a truck. Marines of his platoon and the outfits he had led as a scout mourned a lost comrade.

NICK CARTER

DOG DETECTIVE

MAN is the Bloodhound's natural prey, and Nick Carter tracked down fugitives from the law relentlessly. Some prison-camp Bloodhounds are trained to attack; when they near an escaped convict he climbs a tree in hot haste. Not so Nick--like most of his kind he was mild and gentle. When he found his quarry at the end of a trail, he trotted up to him wagging his tail, as if to say, "Tag, you're it."

Nick was well named after the celebrated dime novel detective, for another title of his ancient breed is Sleuth Hound, and man-hunting has been their specialty since the sixteenth century.

A powerful dog, black and tan with white forehead and chest, Nick Carter's air was alert and he lacked the look of mournful dignity, characteristic of many Bloodhounds. He liked to find lost children, but it was the scent of law-breakers he sniffed oftenest. He established a record when he took and followed a trail 104 hours old. Chalked up to his credit were the trailing, capture, and conviction of 600 criminals. His great achievements did much to restore the public sympathy lost to Bloodhounds by *Uncle Tom's Cabin,* in which they were

Paul Brown

described savagely pursuing the slave "Eliza," fleeing across ice cakes, her baby in her arms.

Nick's master and trainer was the redoubtable Capt. V. G. Mullikan of Kentucky who used the hound in numerous dangerous missions: trailing Hatfield-McCoy feudists, operators of "moonshine" stills, robbers of country stores--trails that might run from ten feet to many miles. Typical was the exploit one day when the owner of a smokehouse saw a thief running from it, fired and missed. A telephone call brought Captain Mullikan, with Nick Carter and his mate, Ivy Bell, in the back of the car, their leashes attached to their collars. Led to the spot where the robber had been sighted, Nick's leash was snapped to his harness. At that signal he took the trail and nosed along it for fifty yards when Ivy Bell replaced him for another fifty. Then the two hounds worked along together, straining at their leashes so that the men found it easier to follow at an eight-mile-an-hour dog-trot than to hold the animals back.

Miles later an isolated cabin loomed through the woods. Mullikan surrounded it with his posse and, hand on his six shooter, strode up to the woman who came to the door. "Step aside," he ordered. Nick and his mate brushed past and went straight up to a certain man in a group at a card game. Though supporting evidence such as shoe and finger prints was gathered, the hounds' identification of the smokehouse robber was accepted in court, as the mute testimony of Bloodhounds often is. Nick Carter, profiting from experience, was a far better tracker in his old age than in his youth. When he died, he was termed "the greatest Bloodhound ever." Swift's lines could serve as his epitaph:

> And though the villain 'scape a while, he feels
> Slow vengeance, like a bloodhound, at his heels.

JESTER

OBEDIENCE CHAMPION

His dam a jet-black Poodle, his sire a pure-white one, Jester, pick of the litter, took after his mother. His curly coat was of the fine texture hoped for from the contrasting colors of his parents. It grew with luxuriance, for Poodles rival Mother Goose's black sheep which furnished three bags full of wool. Given the English saddle clip-bare muzzle and midriff, pom-poms on legs and tail--Jester looked as if he were ready for a carnival or fancy-dress party.

Poodles are born clowns, and Jester lived up to his name. But soon he discovered he was destined for a serious mission. His owners, Blanche Saunders, a pioneer in obedience training, and Louise Branch, expert in animal photography, decided that he was to become a leading demonstrator of disciplined response to orders. Working and sporting dogs long had been taught it, and in recent years its great value had been proved by war dogs and guide dogs for the blind. Its usefulness for all sorts of dogs remained to be shown, and that was to be Jester's job.

Eleven months after his birth in 1944, he won his puppy class in the dog show at Madison Square Garden, New York

City, and placed as a reserve winner (second) in the judging of all male entries. He went on to win other ribbons and to become a champion of his breed, but these were side-issues to his training in obedience.

The big standard Poodle learned manners and the courtesy which makes a gentleman, canine or human. Taught with long patience, rewarded with praise or reprimanded, he was quick to obey when told to sit, stand, lie down, or to stay or to come. He fetched and carried joyfully. For at least a quarter-mile he could track a stranger whose trail was from half an hour to two hours old. When his education was completed, Champion Carillon Jester, to give him his full name, had accumulated an imposing string of degrees: C.D.X. (Companion Dog Excellent), U.D.T. (Utility Dog Tracker), and Int.C.D. (International Companion Dog).

At exhibitions with trained dogs of various other breeds, he cleared high hurdles with graceful leaps; when audiences applauded, Jester would grin, wag his pom-pom and take an encore on his own. He went into the movies as the star of training films. With Miss Saunders he traveled through the United States and Canada, launching obedience classes or demonstrating before gatherings as large as 70,000. He posed for a bronze by the noted sculptress, Malvina Hoffman, and for numerous photographs to illustrate a treatise on training. When that book was brought out, Jester put on one of his best performances to inspire the publisher's salesmen. A veteran on the air, he opened many a radio program on obedience with approving barks. He was an early and popular actor before television cameras. Willing and friendly, he staged shows at veterans' and other hospitals, both an entertainer and a reminder

that training dogs had been a successful healing therapy for the battle-shocked and wounded of the Second World War.

It is an age-old but often forgotten truth that Jester and other obedience-trained dogs have helped make more widely known. Centuries ago the dog gave love and loyalty to man kind, and man in return pledged them to him. That bond becomes closest when dogs are taught to understand how they may serve their masters faithfully and well. For it is through training that man stretches out his hands from across a chasm, as in the legend which begins this book, to grasp the dog leaping the gap to his side.

www.ingramcontent.com/pod-product-compliance
Lightning Source LLC
Chambersburg PA
CBHW022054020426
42335CB00012B/682